The GREAt ADVENTURE.

The GREAT ADVENTURE

HOW GOD TAKES YOU FROM HERE TO THERE

DERRICK C. MOORE

MOODY PUBLISHERS
CHICAGO

Cover image: © 2003 Mark Owen/The Illustration Works

Library of Congress Cataloging-in-Publication Data

Moore, Derrick C.
    The great adventure : how God takes you from here to there / Derrick C. Moore.
      p. cm.
    Includes bibliographical references.
    ISBN 0-8024-1518-0
      1. Conversion—Christianity. 2. Youth—Religious life. I. Title.

BV4921.3.M66 2003
248.4—dc21

2003005723

1 3 5 7 9 10 8 6 4 2

Printed in the United States of America

Dedicated to my wife,
Stephanie Perry Moore,
For your love, support, and vision

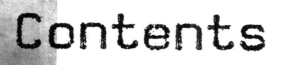

Contents

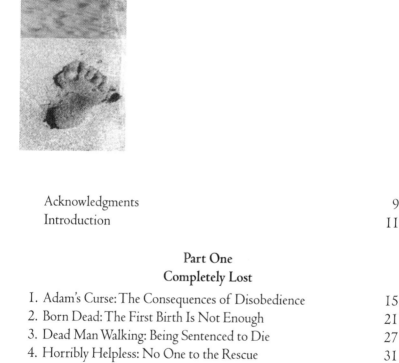

Acknowledgments   9
Introduction   11

Part One
Completely Lost

1. Adam's Curse: The Consequences of Disobedience   15
2. Born Dead: The First Birth Is Not Enough   21
3. Dead Man Walking: Being Sentenced to Die   27
4. Horribly Helpless: No One to the Rescue   31
5. The Stench of Death: Sin Really Does Stink   37
6. When the Death Angel Comes: For Those   41
   Who Don't Know Christ
7. Separated from God: Absolutely No Hope   45

Part Two
Being Found

8. The Voice of God: When He Speaks You'll Know It   51
9. God's Gift of Grace: His Favor Toward Those He Loves   57
10. Ears That Hear: Listen, He's Calling   63
11. Eyes That See: No Longer Blind to the Truth   67
12. Made Alive: We've Been Given New Life   71
13. The Greatest Gift: Thank God for Salvation   75
14. Nothing to Boast About: All Credit Given to God   79

Part Three
Shown the Way

15. The Person Inside: The Incredible Work of the Holy Spirit   85
16. His Workmanship: God's Very Own Masterpiece   89
17. Going to Worship: Why Church Is Important   93
18. A Disciple of Christ: How to Live by the Commands of Christ   97
19. Sharing Our Faith: The Importance of Telling Others About Christ   101
20. The Word of God: Words to Live by   105
21. Time to Pray: Why Prayer Is Important   109

Part Four
Arriving at Home

22. A Family Affair: The Privilege of Being a Family Member   115
23. The Power to Overcome: Being Plugged in to the Power Source   119
24. A Solid Foundation: A Home Fit for the Storm   123
25. The Man of the House: A Father Who Cares   127
26. The Constant Provider: The God Who Meets All Our Needs   131
27. Home Security: The God Who Protects   135
28. And the Greatest of These: The God Whose Motivation Is Love   139

Final Thoughts   143

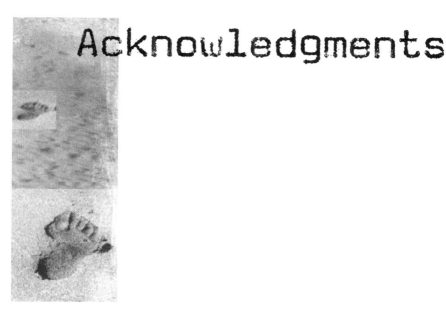

Acknowledgments

It's difficult to put into words my expressions of gratitude to those who helped make this project possible. This book would not exist without some very giving people who truly gave in so many ways.

- Greg Thornton and the Moody Publishers staff, thanks for the opportunity to share Christ.
- Cheryl Dunlop, my editor, thank you for your incredible detail that picked me up when I needed it the most.
- Steve and Carol Shadrach, keep the doors of your home open.
- Curtis Tanner and Campus Outreach Ministries, thank you for showing me how to fish. I've caught some big ones.

- Sid Callaway and the Fellowship of Christian Athletes staff, for your influence in the lives of student athletes all over the world.

- Thank you Chan Gailey, a Christian who happens to be a football coach.

- John Rainey and Randy Roberts, thank you for being faithful.

- Micheal Bunkley, your counsel has been priceless. Thank you for being such a representative of Jesus Christ.

- Dr. E. V. Hill's sermons have inspired and challenged me. He truly was one of the greatest preachers I've ever known. (I was sorry to hear of Dr. Hill's passing while this book was in proofs.)

- To some very dear friends, Kenneth Perry, Byron Johnson, Calvin Cochran, Alonzo Brown, Branson Perry, Antonio London, Cedric Smith, and Anthony Lynn, keep the faith.

- To my parents, Ann Redding (mom), Dr. & Mrs. Franklin Perry Sr. (in laws), your support has made me a better man.

- To my daughters, Sydni and Sheldyn, you are truly a gift from God.

- To my wife, Stephanie, you are so committed to me and my endeavors. I must confess I can't understand why.

- You the reader, I hope you find that a relationship with Jesus Christ is to be desired more than your next breath.

- Last but not least, to Jesus the Christ, I thank You for giving me such a desire to tell others that You are God in the flesh.

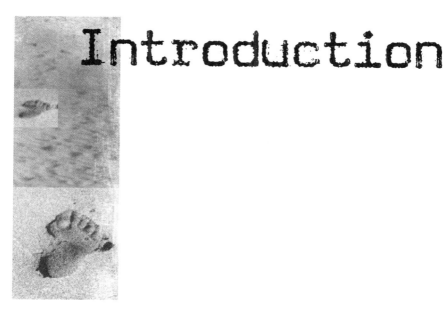

Introduction

Have you ever pondered that life is about getting from one place to another? Whether it's from being a baby to being a teenager, from freshman year to senior year, or from school to work, every day we are on some adventure. In sports, track athletes go from start to finish, football players travel from one end zone to the other, and golf starts on hole one and ends at hole eighteen. Can you see the pattern? Sometimes we don't know how to accomplish what we need. We are unsure which road to go down. Life often leaves us with one of its most mind-staggering questions, How do we get from here to there? We need someone to help us find our way.

As we voyage through *The Great Adventure*, I will show you how a person can go from being separated from God to being reunited with God. Part I, "Completely Lost," focuses on man in his most miserable state. Part 2, "Being Found," deals with a God who sees you lost and extends His love to you by seeking you out. Part 3, "Shown the Way," highlights God taking you by the hand and showing you how to walk with Him. And finally Part 4, "Arriving at Home," helps you understand the bond every believer has as a member of God's family.

It is my hope that you will enjoy and experience the wonderful journey of traveling from here, being completely lost, to there, at home where you belong. It is the greatest adventure the human heart will ever know. Come and walk it with me.

PART ONE

Completely Lost
Living a Meaningless Life

As for you, you were dead in your transgressions and sins.
-EPHESIANS 2:1

Can you imagine going to college and studying a difficult curriculum that requires countless hours of time and work, only to discover that there is no degree awaiting you at the completion of your studies? Or can you imagine being an athlete training hard for an athletic event, only to find that despite your efforts you still were not in shape? Or what about walking all the way to the kitchen or the cafeteria, only to discover there is no food?

Then can you imagine living on earth for eighty years only to discover at the end of your life that everything you did had no real meaning or value? The world is filled with people young and old, rich and poor, smart and not so smart who are living meaningless lives. I want to share with you in this section why life is meaningless apart from being in a relationship with Jesus Christ.

I know you thought you were walking and actually going somewhere; maybe you're the big man on campus, or maybe you're a homecoming queen, or maybe you're even a straight-A student. Maybe you've just been accepted into a fine college, or maybe you just got your first real job and it pays twice what you were expecting. All of those things are great. However, if Jesus Christ is not Lord and Savior of your life, then even though you are moving, you are moving on a treadmill, going nowhere. Walk with me in this first part and see how awful it is to be completely lost.

CHAPTER ONE

Adam's Curse

The Consequences of Disobedience

Through the disobedience of the one man the many were made sinners.
—ROMANS 5:19

I know you're pretty much on your own now. In college or doing your thing. Maybe you're in the workforce earning your way. More or less living by your own rules. But can you think back with me for a moment to when you weren't so independent, back to the days when the folks whose house you lived in set all the rules?

Do you remember when your parents told you not to do something and you did it anyway, or when they told you to do something and you didn't do it? Come on, you remember at least one time when you didn't obey.

"Don't take the cookies from the cookie jar." *I'll just sneak about three.* "Don't turn the TV on after 10:00." *It's only 11:00 P.M., and channel surfing will help me get to sleep.* "Don't leave for school without making your bed." *Making the bed, ha, that's a joke.* "Put your things up." *Oh, there's a place for all that stuff in my room.* "Fold your clothes." *If I stuff them in a drawer, Mom will never know.* "Make sure you register next week for the SAT." *I'll take the next one; I'm not ready.* Any of that sound familiar?

Whatever was asked of you, there were probably several times you didn't obey. As a result of your disobedience, severe consequences entered your world, I'm sure. Simple instructions with incorrect responses sometimes lead to disaster.

If you're like me, you've disobeyed your parents on many occasions. Now let me set the record straight. I was not mischievous. I just had my own agenda as a youngster from time to time. For example, riding my bicycle with friends was way more important than taking the trash out. When I was twelve years old, two of my good buddies asked me to go riding with them. I knew I hadn't done what my mom asked of me, and I was about to say I couldn't go when they said, "Come on, D, we'll be back way before your mama gets home. You can take out the trash when we get back. Don't miss all the fun." Now the pondering begins. Trash or fun? I'm sure you know what I chose.

Let me tell you about one particular student who had some similar choices. He had just completed his senior year of high school, and his mind was set on taking his future to the next level. He was a bright kid with high ambitions. His excitement for college led him to pack weeks before it was time to leave. As the summer came to an end, the anticipation of becoming a college student mounted. All that was left to do was for his parents to drive him to the university campus.

His mother and father had a conversation with him as they made their way to the university campus he was scheduled to attend for the next four years. The father opened the conversation by saying, "Son, I know you are excited about your first year in college. Your mom and I have looked forward to this day for quite some time; however, we would like to talk to you about our expectations. We want you to understand the danger of making poor decisions and losing sight of your purpose. College is a place to get an outstanding education and discover new relationships. However, there are also many distractions that can sidetrack you from your goals, such as all-night parties, staying up late doing the wrong things, and not devoting enough time to your studies."

When his father finished talking, the son squirmed in the backseat of the car. You know he was uncomfortable. No one likes getting the third degree. The warnings weren't over as his mother began to speak. "We expect you to live by the rules and standards of the institution. We expect you to go to class, pay attention, study, and have a complete understanding of what your priorities should be while in college. It is our desire to see you graduate in four years. Your father and I want you to fulfill your purpose of getting an education. If you don't, the doors of opportunity will close, and it will take a miracle to open them again."

There was complete silence from the son after his parents finished what they had to say. He finally responded by saying, "I understand, and you have nothing to worry about."

After the first semester the son finished with a C, one D, and three Fs. It wasn't a very enjoyable ride home for Christmas break. Determined to improve his academic performance, he returned to school with a seemingly new attitude. But the results were the same. Needless to say, he disobeyed the instructions given by his parents. He was expelled due to inadequate academic performance in his first year of enrollment.

Later he told his parents his experiences during his first year in college. First he talked about the enormous amount of freedom he had. "Mom and Dad, you have to understand, my classes on some days end at 11:00. Some days I don't have to go to some of my classes. It's not like high school, where you had to attend each subject every day." Second, he said the girls were a major distraction. "Dad, you understand what happens during the spring semester. Some of these girls walk around in their short shorts and tight miniskirts." He finally confessed to losing sight of his purpose and disobeying his parents' instructions.

The same can be said for Adam. Adam was God's first created human being. "God created man in his own image, in the image of God he created him" (Genesis 1:27). Adam was placed in a garden called Eden and was given a purpose to cultivate it and keep it (Genesis 2:15). God gave Adam permission to eat from any tree of the garden except from the Tree of Knowledge of Good and Evil. He told him, "You must not eat from the tree of the knowledge of good and evil, for when you eat of it you will surely die" (Genesis 2:17). Not adhering to the warning by his Father, Adam ate of the forbidden fruit, and like falling dominos he set off a chain reaction that has fallen all the way to you and me.

Like the college son, Adam agreed to his father's terms. And unfortunately, like the college son, Adam failed to comply.

You've heard the story, but can't you see beautiful Eve telling Adam it was OK to disobey God? Saying the right thing, looking the right way, tempting him till he gave in. The fruit probably tasted delicious, but I'm sure that the second bite for Adam was sour in more ways than one. I wonder, during that second bite, did he realize he'd blown it? Did Adam know that he'd messed it up for us all?

I know that he and Eve realized that they were naked, which is why they covered themselves. But I seriously doubt that he realized his act of disobedience would affect every generation of people to come. Whether Adam knew it or not, the consequence of his disobedience was the curse of sin and man's ultimate separation from God. Romans 6:23 says, "For the wages of sin is death." Adam disobeyed the rules and standards God had for him. God's simple instructions somehow got lost in the moment. It is now because of this one man Adam that the whole world has been sentenced to death.

Romans 5:14 (NKJV) says, "Nevertheless death reigned from Adam to Moses, even over those who had not sinned according to the likeness of the transgression of Adam, who is a type of Him who was to come." Adam by his sin brought ruin to the human race.

The opportunity to get a higher education for one college student went down the tubes because of his disobedience. The whole world is in ruin because of disobedience. The price of disobeying can really be costly. I understand how hard it is to resist temptation when it comes after you. But is giving in to it worth it? When my friends came by the day I was supposed to take out the trash, they persuaded me to join them right away. Trash could wait. So that's what I did. I did not want to miss any fun. Well, the end of that story was that I was grounded for a week. I ended up missing even more fun because of my disobedience. Riding with my friends before my chores were done wasn't worth it.

Adam's sin wasn't worth it. It cost him and everyone after him a harmonious relationship with God. It has cost many people eternal separation from God. How much are you willing to pay for an act of disobedience?

CHAPTER TWO

Born Dead

The First Birth Is Not Enough

Jesus declared, "I tell you the truth, no one can see the kingdom of God unless he is born again."
—JOHN 3:3

I know what you're thinking. *What an unusual title. How can a person be born dead? What kind of sense does that make, Mr. Moore?*

Now, I have a great level of respect for your intelligence. Nevertheless, this oxymoron of a title can't be intellectualized. There you go thinking again, trying to figure out what in the world I'm talking about. No need to strain your brain. Come closer, I'll explain.

On the college campus, each student is given a core curriculum to complete for graduation. The curriculum is spread out over a span of four or five years, or even six or seven years for those who just *love* the college campus. When I was in college, I had the dubious task of passing chemistry, which was required in order to graduate.

Again, I know what you are thinking. You're thinking, *Hey, chemistry is easy.* You can't believe that I struggled to pass it. Well, I did, thank you very much. As a matter of fact, I struggled so badly I failed the course. All those atoms and molecules completely confused me. The only compound element I understood was H_2O. Growing up in the smoldering summer temperatures of the South will give a person a great appreciation for water. To me that horrible class was my worst nightmare. I thought I'd never wake up from that nightmare called "chemistry." I realized that if I was going to complete the curriculum, I had to pass the class.

I imagine that you can relate to my experience—hearing the teacher lecture on material that you do not comprehend on any level. You study and study, and no improvement is made. You write your notes over, and they still aren't any help. So you borrow someone else's notes hoping he got something you missed, and to no avail—you're still not getting it. Then you talk to the professor, scared to admit to him or her that his or her teaching methods are way over your head, in hopes that the professor could break it down in elementary terms. When that doesn't work, there's but one option left—you drop the class.

Maybe it wasn't a science course for you. Maybe it was a subject in business, psychology, history, math, or literature. Whatever it was, if you didn't pass it, you wouldn't complete the curriculum until you did. Unless, of course, you knew something I didn't.

Ever hear of someone in the Bible named Nicodemus? Well, if you haven't, let me get you acquainted with who he was. And if you have heard of this wise old teacher, please bear with me a moment. Nicodemus was an accomplished teacher of the synagogues, the religious teaching centers of Israel. He was highly regarded as a Pharisee. He was intelligent and extremely familiar with the law. I can see him now, proud that his thoughts were rarely challenged, if at all. Folks in his town were that confident in his ability to know stuff. Think about the professor that everyone knows is the smartest. Well, that would be a Nicodemus type.

His encounter with Jesus was historic and life changing. It is recorded in John 3:2 that Nicodemus encountered Jesus at night. Why? I don't really know. My guess would be Mr. "I have all the answers" didn't want anyone to see him talking to Jesus. Why should he need to ask anyone anything? And especially why should he ask anything of Jesus, whom his fellow teachers thought was a dangerous teacher? Those could be logical questions for the townspeople if they knew what their Pharisee was up to.

But only Nicodemus knew his heart. He had something weighing on it very heavily that night. He needed to speak to Jesus to clear up a few things.

Have you ever had something on your mind that bothered you so badly you couldn't sleep? You just could not rest until you got it off your chest. Well, that's how I can envision this man feeling. Finally, they're all alone. Jesus, who had proclaimed Himself to be Savior of the world, on one side of the table, and Nicodemus, the great intellectual on Bible law, on the other.

Nicodemus fires away. "Rabbi, we know you are a teacher who has come from God. For no one could perform the miraculous signs you are doing if God were not with him" (John 3:2). Jesus sticks to the point. He explains to Nicodemus that he has failed the course, and unless he takes it again, he cannot complete the curriculum. All his spiritual knowledge isn't enough, and he has missed the main point. I know Nicodemus was even more confused at this point.

Nicodemus had failed to understand that his physical birth was insufficient for him to enter into the kingdom of God. Jesus was trying to tell him that he needed a spiritual birth. Jesus said, "Truly, truly, I say to you, unless one is born of water and the Spirit he cannot enter into the kingdom of God. That which is born of the flesh is flesh, and that which is born of the Spirit is spirit" (John 3:5–6 NASB). Jesus made plain to Nicodemus that there is no getting around it. The eternal fact of life is that a person *must* be born again.

Ephesians 2:1 reveals further evidence that the new birth is necessary to a relationship with God. "You were dead in your transgressions and sins." What this really means is that you were born into sin because of the sin of Adam. There was nothing Nicodemus could do in and of himself to change that fact. There is nothing you can do to change that fact either.

Nicodemus, while seeking answers, began asking Jesus questions about the new birth. Some of the questions may sound dumb, but the only way to find the answers was to ask the questions. If you don't know, you just don't know.

I know that sometimes there are questions that you want to ask in class that seem dumb, but I encourage you to ask them. Knowing the answers can mean the difference between passing and failing and between understanding and not understanding. For Nicodemus, it meant the difference between life and death.

Thank God for Nicodemus's sake that he asked the questions and Jesus provided the answers. Nicodemus asked three life-changing questions. "How can a man be born when he is old?" Without letting Jesus answer the first question, an extremely confused Nicodemus asked a second question, "He cannot enter a second time into his mother's womb and be born, can he?" (John 3:4, all NASB). This is when Jesus answered, "Truly,

truly, I say to you, unless one is born of water and the Spirit he cannot enter into the kingdom of God" (v. 5). Still confused, Nicodemus asked, "How can these things be?" (v. 9). Jesus responded, "Are you the teacher of Israel and do not understand these things?" (v. 10). Nicodemus asked the questions and Jesus provided the answers.

Such has been the case not only for Nicodemus but throughout the Bible as well. Hurting, lost, sick, and depraved people all had questions for the Savior, questions that only He could answer. And wow, did He have the answers! "For God so loved the world, that he gave his one and only son, that whoever believes in him shall not perish but have eternal life" (John 3:16).

After taking my chemistry class a second time, I passed. If you ever failed a course or didn't succeed the first time, you probably had more success the second time around. After Nicodemus talked with Jesus a while, I believe he really understood the new birth. It wasn't a physical thing at all, like being born the first time. Rather, it was a new relationship with God through Jesus Christ—being born not of one's mother, but of the Holy Spirit.

I truly hope that *you* understand the new birth. Well, that leaves one more question to be answered. Not a question for your parents. Not a question for your friends. But a question for you: Do you believe you must be born again?

CHAPTER THREE

Dead Man Walking

Being Sentenced to Die

For the wages of sin is death.
—ROMANS 6:23a

You've heard the expression "If the shoe fits, wear it," haven't you? Just imagine being in a shoe store and heading straight for the row of shoes that are your size. You might see several pairs you like. So you begin to try them on, pair after pair. I'm certain not every shoe in your size is something you'd wear. The shoe may be ugly, too cheap, too expensive, the wrong color, uncomfortable, or simply not to your taste. And if the shoe happens to fall into one of these categories, though it fits, you wouldn't wear it. Sin fits you and me like a brand-new pair of shoes. But just because it fits doesn't mean we have to wear it.

Go with me to a college campus. Let's check out people walking about with no appetite for the things of God. Their spiritual taste buds are dead. Anything holy is as bland to them

as food is to a person with the flu. Therefore they can't taste the goodness of almighty God.

Their days are filled with fraternity or sorority parties where everyone leaves a little toasted. Athletics and campus politics have become their gods. Some of them have to be the center of attention and will do whatever it takes to make that happen: steroids, lying, drugs, backstabbing, etc. The thrill of pursuing the American dream has become their passion. Wrongly believing that only the rich and ruthless survive, these are the walking dead. They are physically alive, but spiritually dead. Dead man walking! I may have described you. And if so, please keep reading.

Years ago, when I was in college (yep, I said years ago, but not *that* many, thank you kindly), I had a friend who was the best defensive football player in the history of our school. He held the sack record, was very popular, was about to graduate, and had his pick of the girls. In his eyes, what else did a guy need? I knew he didn't have Jesus Christ, so I was on a mission to get him saved.

A church in a nearby town was having a revival. I knew the speaker for the week was excellent. Even if my friend turned me down, I was going to ask him to go. To my surprise, he agreed to go, though I could tell by his hesitation that he didn't want to go.

He didn't think the tall preacher with a receding hairline, dressed in a black robe, could tell him anything of interest. At first he sat in the church bored. But when the preacher began to speak on the subject of death, his slumped shoulders straightened up. I could see that the preacher had his attention.

At that point in his life he saw himself as pretty important. *He* was the man in his life. *He* had gotten himself an opportunity to walk on the football team. *He* impressed the coaches enough to obtain a full scholarship. *He* made plays and stood out among all the defensive players. No one else did those things but him. Or so he thought.

The preacher told us that because of Adam's sin we were all sentenced to die. He said, "I know you don't see yourselves as dead people walking, but if you have never had your sins forgiven in a personal way through Jesus Christ, you indeed are a dead man walking." Due to the fact that Adam sinned in the Garden, his sin became our sin. Later my friend confessed to me that he'd never heard it put into quite those terms.

After learning of his condition, he was ready to repent. With his hands sweating and his heart racing, he knew he truly didn't want to be characterized as a dead man walking.

Did you get a chance to see the movie *The Green Mile?* I discussed it vividly with some college students at a Christmas conference. Tom Hanks played the prison guard in charge of inmates on death row. Michael Clarke Duncan played a huge mountain of a man accused of killing two little girls and sentenced to die because of what they thought he did.

When the time came for the inmates to be executed, the prison guards would yell the most dreadful words imaginable, "Dead man walking!" One of the college students admitted that seeing this movie was the closest he'd ever come to understanding the condition we are all in apart from receiving Jesus Christ.

Found in Luke 23 is the account of the crucifixion of the two thieves who died to the left and to the right of Jesus. The two were convicted and sentenced to die by crucifixion.

These were two men who deserved what they received. "We are punished justly, for we are getting what our deeds deserve," said one (Luke 23:41). At least they knew that they had a death sentence because of their crimes. Many today don't know their fate apart from receiving Jesus Christ as Lord and Savior. Don't be that person.

Do you know that there is a God with whom you once were in a right relationship through Adam? Do you know that through Adam your relationship with God was broken? Do you know that through this broken relationship you have been sentenced to death? Do you recognize your own choice to go your own way rather than God's way? Well, if you didn't know, you know now.

The next few years will shape your views of the world, others, and yourself. You will develop convictions, be they good or bad, right or wrong. Before you know it, the years of young adulthood will have come and gone. The most important thing you can learn is not history or English or any other subject or major. The most important knowledge you can acquire is to know whether or not you're still on death row.

You and I have sinned. We have gone our own way. We have done our own thing. We have lived as if God doesn't exist. But I've got good news: If you are on death row, you can get off.

CHAPTER FOUR

Horribly Helpless

No One to the Rescue

For while we were still helpless, at the right time Christ died for the ungodly.
—ROMANS 5:6 (NASB)

The first lesson I learned in college was that I was no longer in high school. You remember high school, don't you? Mom and Dad were there to wake you for school. Mom prepared the most scrumptious breakfasts. Ah, homemade biscuits, delicious pancakes, and mouthwatering omelets. Nothing like Mom's cooking. All the conveniences of parental assistance when you need it.

Once you're in college, the perks you enjoyed in high school take on a whole new meaning. For instance, if you want to make it to class on time and sneak in a little breakfast as well, you'd better learn how to wake yourself up on time. And by the way, breakfast on the college campus can get to be a bit discouraging after you've had it a few times. Everyone for himself. Personal responsibility, high expectations, and very few excuses accepted.

During 1995, I had the privilege of playing professional

football for the Carolina Panthers. This was the inaugural season for the expansion team. One particular weekend we were flying to Foxboro, Massachusetts, to play the New England Patriots. The entire team of players, coaches, and management was aboard the chartered flight.

As we got close to our destination, the plane experienced the most frightening turbulence I have ever encountered. The airplane felt as if it were falling from the sky. Those big NFL players were being tossed around, scrumptious food was spilled everywhere, and screams were coming from every direction. There I was, the starting running back, curled up in a fetal position, praying and hoping we would make it. I could do nothing to change the condition we were in.

My life flashed before my eyes. I thought I'd never see my pretty Southern belle again. I didn't think I'd ever taste my mama's cubed steak and rice again. And I just knew I'd never touch an end zone again.

I had no control over what was going to happen next. I had to depend on a pilot I'd never met to save my life and the lives of my friends. I was completely helpless.

Finally, the aircraft stopped shaking. My teammates stopped screaming. And the pilot announced that things were under control. We landed safely at the airport. Whew!

While on staff with a ministry called Campus Outreach, I was the spiritual mentor for a student named John. His transition from high school to college certainly was an eye-opening experience. John had been so accustomed to living in his comfort zone called high school (you know, the big man on campus, everybody knew his name, football superstar) that he was completely overwhelmed with this new place called college. Questions flooded his mind. "Where is Mom? Where is Dad? Who are these people? Where are my high school friends? Where can I get some money? What about my laundry?" Everywhere were unfamiliar faces and unfamiliar places. John had no clue that at first he'd be so helpless.

I know you've been there. Feeling horribly helpless with no one to the rescue. Can you remember how you felt when you first got to high school or college? Afraid? Or lonely? Or possibly even helpless? Not a very good feeling, is it?

John once told me about the awful experience of taking his first big psychology test. He had spent the entire weekend with his friends, playing basketball, watching TV, and relaxing. He only put in a few minutes of study time, and he thought that it would be enough to prepare himself for the exam, only he found out it wasn't. Monday morning during the exam he felt completely helpless as he suffered through the test, and he failed miserably.

Bet you've been down that road before. Have you ever felt helpless when faced with enormous temptation? Ever wonder why you can't kick a bad habit that seems to take control of your life? Or is there anger in your life that seems to change your personality? If you're honest with yourself, being helpless is an experience you've had at one time or another, the feeling that there is nothing you can do to bring these agonizing emotions under control.

One of my favorite stories in the Bible is when Peter is trying to walk on water to get over to Jesus (Matthew 14:22–31). This whole walking-on-water thing intrigues me. I mean I can see Jesus walking on water. He's God's Son. Surely Peter didn't think he could do what Jesus did. Right?

Wrong! Peter fooled me. He asked the Savior if he could walk on water, and when given the go-ahead to try, he stepped

out of the boat and successfully walked a few feet alone. But when Peter took his eyes off Jesus, he became frightened and began to sink.

If that had been me, I would have thought it was over. I would have known I was about to drown. But Peter, though helpless, called for Jesus. Peter knew that without His assistance, he was in deep trouble.

A few of my favorite verses in the Bible confirm we are all horribly helpless apart from Jesus Christ. Romans 5:6 says, "For while we were still *helpless,* at the right time Christ died for the ungodly" (NASB, italics added). *Helpless* here means there is nothing you or I could do about our condition. We were separated from God due to Adam's sin and our own. Horribly separated, because our fate is death. That means eternal death—separation from God forever—not just that someday we will die of cancer or heart disease or in a car accident.

Romans 6:23 says, "For the wages of sin is death." We are helpless, because in and of ourselves there is nothing we can do to change this condition. Ephesians 2:8–9 says, "For it is by grace you have been saved, through faith—and this not from yourselves, it is the gift of God—not by works, so that no one can boast."

Romans 5:12 says, "Sin entered the world through one man, and death through sin, and in this way death came to all men, because all sinned." The one man here, whereby sin spread, is Adam. Adam represents condemnation. That means you and I stand condemned to a state of helplessness, unable to do anything in and of ourselves about our condition.

On that airplane, I was helpless. When John didn't study for his test, he was helpless. When Peter was sinking in the water, you guessed it, he also was helpless. Three men in different situations, all desperately needing to be rescued.

My favorite types of films are action movies. Most of the time, the hero has to rescue the damsel in distress. Sometimes the woman is trapped in a room, with the building on fire, screaming for help. Or she may be chained to a railroad track, with the powerful locomotive approaching, yelling for assistance. Or the woman is tied up, about to be bitten by a venomous snake, calling for the hero. Take a moment to reflect on these three images of being horribly helpless and consider that is you in the burning building, or that's you tied to the railroad track, or that's you about to be bitten by the venomous snake. Without Christ you are horribly helpless and unable to do anything about your condition.

God considers you to be His damsel in distress. You are in distress because of Adam, who sinned through disobedience, and because of your own choice to do things your way rather than God's way. Now the residue of Adam's sin has left you, me, and the entire world horribly helpless. Don't you want to be rescued? The hero is but a prayer away.

CHAPTER FIVE

The Stench of Death

Sin Really Does Stink

For all have sinned and fall short of the glory of God.
—ROMANS 3:23

Hold your breath. Cover your nostrils. You won't like the smell of this chapter.

I hate to take you inside the locker room after a college football game, but go with me there for a minute. Musty jerseys, stinky socks, grimy pants, and smelly players—wow, what an odor! Everyone in the room is most certainly in need of a shower. Can you smell the stench? Well, that's just how bad I believe sin stinks to our heavenly Father.

In the neighborhood I lived in as a kid, we had a terrible problem with the sewage one winter. Folks couldn't walk the street without covering their nostrils. The city's sewage and waste department sent many trucks out to fix the problem. To those who lived in the neighborhood, their visits didn't fix the problem . . . they made it worse. Finally the sewage got so backed up that it burst. Waste poured onto the street, and the stench overwhelmed the neighborhood. Until the problem was fixed, every resident was exposed to the smell. Even though the sewage was in the back of the neighborhood, the people in the front could smell the stench as much as the people in the back could. Sin is the same way. Not some of us, but all of us, have sinned, and the stench overwhelms everything.

I once asked several students what were some of their favorite games. Some said playing cards, others said pool, some enjoyed video games, and the game of throwing darts was even among the favorites. I learned that throwing darts is one of the more exciting games, because it requires a bit of skill and a very steady hand. The dartboard is placed about eight to ten feet in front of the players. The goal is to hit the bull's-eye, the center of the board. Many times I watched as student after student tried and no one hit the center.

Sin can be described as missing the bull's-eye. No matter how good you are or how many nice things you do, you and I have missed the bull's-eye. Through Adam sin entered the world, and its stench can be smelled everywhere.

Taken from the gospel according to John is the story of the death and resurrection of Lazarus. Lazarus had two sisters, sweet Mary and serving Martha. They lived in a place called Bethany. It was a quiet little country town. Not too much ever happened there.

We are told that Lazarus became sick. Concerned for their brother, Mary and Martha frantically sent word to Jesus. Using a phrase that probably describes an exceptionally close relationship Jesus had with Lazarus, the sisters sent word to Jesus that said, "The one you love is sick" (John 11:3).

Hearing of Lazarus' condition, Jesus remained where He

was. He didn't go running to Bethany to save His friend. He didn't stay for lack of concern but out of obedience to the Father. Understand that God is painting a picture of His miraculous power to raise the dead so that the Father may be glorified.

Jesus said in John 11:4 that Lazarus' sickness was not to end in death, but it was for the glory of God. At least four long days would pass before Jesus made His way to where Lazarus was. By the time Jesus arrived, Lazarus had died, and Mary and Martha were discouraged. When Jesus asked them to roll back the stone from Lazarus' tomb, Martha replied, "By this time there is a bad odor, for he has been there four days" (John 11:39).

I must confess that I don't know what a four-day-old dead body smells like, but I would imagine it's the most awful smell there is. Combine the smell of a skunk, a rotten onion, and cow manure, and you might be close. But even imagining that unpleasant concoction pales in comparison to the smell of sin in the nostrils of God.

Man's worst condition is sin. Not the loss of his possessions, or the loss of health, or the loss of loved ones. It's sin, the stench that has penetrated the life of every human being both past and present. The account of Genesis 2 tells us that man was once in perfect fellowship with God. But because of his rebellion and disobedience, sin entered the world. Romans 3:23 says that all have sinned and fallen short of the glory of God. That means you and I have fallen below God's intended purpose for His creation, thereby creating a great gulf between God and man.

Sometimes we use a picture of two giant cliffs with a deep valley between to illustrate that a holy God stands on one side of the gulf and sinful man on the other. The gulf represents sin or the condition man is in. A significant verse communicates the effect that sin has on human existence: "For the wages of sin is death" (Romans 6:23)—meaning if you spend your time in sin and live according to sin, its payment will be death.

So if you are wondering whether or not you have a sin problem, wonder no more. It may be stealing, lying, fornicating, or cheating, or it may be none of those things. But you have one. We all have one. And sin is a smell that God hates—a stench that's so great that God had to send His only Son, Jesus Christ, to take away the smell.

Remember that Romans 6:23 doesn't end with "the wages of sin is death." We are also given hope with the word *but*. Fortunately, that Scripture goes on to say, "But the gift of God is eternal life in Christ Jesus our Lord." A gift has been prepared for you. All you have to do is receive it. Then things will smell a whole lot better, and you can uncover your nostrils, take a deep breath, and enjoy the sin-free, fresh smelling air. Sin-free fresh smelling air? *What does that smell like?* you might ask. I imagine it to be much better than the combined smell of hot apple pie, a bouquet of lilies, and the morning air after an all-night rain. Go ahead, take a sniff.

CHAPTER SIX

When the Death Angel Comes

For Those Who Don't Know Christ

When the Lamb opened the fourth seal,
I heard the voice of the fourth living
creature say, "Come!" I looked, and
there before me was a pale horse! Its
rider was named Death, and Hades was
following close behind him. They were
given power over a fourth of the earth
to kill by sword, famine and plague, and
by the wild beasts of the earth.

—REVELATION 6:7–8

Get ready, get ready, here it comes, are you ready? *What's coming?* you might ask. Well, the end of the world. You didn't think this was home, did you?

During my days as a professional football player, I looked forward to the start of each football season. Cheering fans, pregame music, road trips, and the thrill of taking the field for battle always got me pumped. However, before any of those things could happen, I had to endure the agony of what is called training camp. It is the most miserable place on earth. Very early morning practices, draining afternoon practices, aching muscles, smoldering temperatures, and the constant drive of the taskmasters (better known as the football coaches).

Let me give you a few snapshots of the experience of two-a-days. The first order of business is to make sure that all the reporting players are in the best of health. Therefore a physical is required for all the players. The physical can start as early as 5:00 A.M. with a urine test. An EKG is given to examine the heart. A blood pressure exam and blood test are given, and the athlete also makes a visit to the orthopedic surgeon to examine bones, muscles, and ligaments. All of these things happen to ensure the safety of the players. The physicals can last several hours and sometimes can seem endless. Uniforms are distributed to each player. Team meetings are scheduled for later that evening. Finally, when all players are cleared for practice, it becomes survival of the fittest.

The toil that training camp takes on the body and the mind can best be described as hell on earth. The body is sore from head to toe, and the mind is stretched to its ultimate limits. There are usually two practices a day for two weeks, or if you are on the professional level, two-a-days can last three or four weeks, most of which takes place in almost unbearable heat.

When training camp ends, some have survived; others have succumbed. The agony and torture of two-a-days can be overwhelming. For a player, when this time of the year comes, he had better try to be as prepared as possible. For those on the pro level who are not prepared, the end result is being released from the team—no longer employed.

Years ago Hurricane Andrew hit Florida with devastating winds and destructive forces. Homes were destroyed, businesses were ruined, schools were leveled, and lives were lost. The arrival of Andrew so devastated the economy that it left Floridians in a state of emergency.

Remarkably, some were not affected. Smart people made preparations by boarding up their properties. A vast majority were safe from the storm because they left the area. When nature strikes we don't always have a warning. However, for this particular hurricane, the word was out. Those who heeded the call were glad they complied. Those who didn't, you can only imagine the pain and anguish they felt over not being ready.

The Bible tells us in Exodus 12:12 that in the days of Moses God sent the death angel through the land of Egypt. God executed judgment by killing all of the firstborn in the land. To protect His people, God instructed Moses to tell the people to spread blood over the doors of all of those who belonged to the house of Israel. In all those houses that did not have the blood over their doors, the death angel would come and strike down the firstborn.

Death and destruction are subjects we do not enjoy talking about. However, it is necessary to discuss them because of the reality of the difficult times ahead for those who don't know Jesus Christ. According to biblical teaching, you and I will spend eternity either with Christ or without Christ. We will either prepare for eternity by receiving Jesus Christ, or we will slip into eternity having never received Christ. We all will spend eternity somewhere. The question then is, Where will it be? Your eternity could start this very hour. Are you prepared to enter into eternity? Or are you like so many who never prepared themselves for what is to come?

The only way to prepare for eternity is to know Jesus Christ, God's only Son, as Savior and Lord. There is no other shelter, no other way, and no other solution. What's coming in the future is beyond human comprehension.

Don't you want the death angel to pass over you? I was glad I was prepared for training camp. That's how I survived. The Floridians who survived Andrew were glad they prepared for the hurricane. The Israelites were prepared because of the blood. Don't you want to be prepared for what's to come? If so, the Lamb has been slain, and His blood can be poured over your doorpost. In plain English, Jesus is the Lamb who has been killed, and His blood can protect you from the death your sins deserve if you ask Him to protect you with His blood.

CHAPTER SEVEN

Separated from God

Absolutely No Hope

Surely the arm of the LORD is not too short to save, nor his ear too dull to hear. But your iniquities have separated you from your God; your sins have hidden his face from you, so that he will not hear.

—ISAIAH 59:1–2

I can only imagine the horror of being separated from someone who loves me more than I love myself. I know what you're saying: "No one loves me more than I love myself." Perhaps you think you're the best thing since sliced bread, and it can't be possible that someone loves you more than you do. Well, there is. But there's only one problem. Because of everything said in the previous chapters, you have been separated from the Creator of heaven and earth. What can be more horrific?

I remember visiting a major theme park in Ohio when it was packed with thousands of visitors—men, women, and children from all over the country. And with all the people, it seemed to take forever to ride anything.

Can you imagine being five years old and separated from your parents in such an environment? Well, it happened to five-year-old

Tommy. He was a cute little fellow. Blond hair, blue eyes, cowboy hat, and a sticky blue face from the cotton candy he was eating. Somehow he got separated from his parents. One moment he was standing with Dad; the next he was surrounded by a crowd of strangers. Lost among thousands of people, not knowing if he would see his parents again, he just started sobbing.

I was moved by what I saw next. The theme park security officer quickly held little Tommy and began to comfort him. At the same time, he got on his walkie-talkie and started to radio in for help. The search began for Tommy's parents.

I wanted to do whatever I could to help. So I stayed with the theme park security officer and Tommy until his folks were found. Fortunately, after thirty minutes of searching and praying, Tommy's parents were found. It was a joy to see him reunited with the people he loved.

Tommy's hope was in the effort of the theme park security officer to locate his parents. Fortunately for Tommy, he did. The Bible tells us that the separation from God is not temporal but eternal for those who don't know Jesus Christ as Savior. There will be no one there to look for you. No one to hold your hand. And no one to give you comforting words. There is absolutely no hope for those who die and leave this life having never made Jesus Christ their Lord and Savior.

From the time that you were born, you were provided for and nurtured by someone. Remember all the fun you had: birthday parties, family vacations, holiday celebrations, and, most important, I know you probably remember the comforting arms of Mom, Dad, or whoever raised you. They were always there to love you and help you. You're a young adult now. Far gone are those days, but I bet you remember.

Now can you imagine all of that gone? No birthday cakes,

no pictures at Disneyland, and no Christmas dinner. It's no fun being separated from the ones who love you.

Sara was about to start her senior year at Yale University. The past three years, her father had taken her to school. He made sure she had everything she needed before he left his youngest daughter on the campus. The week before they were to venture on their last trip to the school, her dad told her how excited he was for the journey. He also expressed his joy over Sara's accomplishments. The day after their heartfelt chat, Sara's dad had a massive heart attack and passed away.

Sara was strong during the time that the family dealt with her father's passing. It wasn't until she drove herself to school alone that she realized she'd never see her dad on earth again. You can surely empathize with the deep sense of loss she felt. She was devastated over the fact that he was gone.

Holding on to the memories got her through. As she drove to Yale in a quiet car, she laughed most of the way at the funny things she remembered her dad saying. Though they were apart, he was in her heart. She also came to the sad fact that her father was not a Christian. Sara had accepted Jesus Christ, but her father had not. She could only weep as she thought about never seeing him again.

Every Easter, I reread the story of the Cross. Every year after reading it, I feel full, like I've eaten the biggest meal of my life. One of my favorite parts of the story is the part about the thief on the cross (Luke 23:39–43).

Can't you see the guy who actually deserved to be there? He was a robber and a murderer. He was surely destined for hell. I'm sure as he hung there, he heard the fiery flames calling his name.

But sometime after he was nailed to a cross like Jesus, he wanted to know Jesus. He realized in his last moments on earth that though they had the same cruel death, they didn't have the same hope. Jesus was destined to return to heaven. The thief was destined for hell. In a matter of minutes, he would be eternally separated from God.

The frightened thief did what he could to make himself a place with the Father. He asked Jesus to remember him. The Son of God agreed. The thief's last few words saved him from being separated from God. I bet after Jesus reassured the thief that he'd spend eternity with God, he had peace.

I must confess that I can't comprehend what being separated from God really means, but Scripture says that it means *forever and forever and forever.* No hope forever. No light forever, no love forever. Never being united with the One who loves you the most. Oh, how frightening that must be.

I alluded to the horror in the beginning of the chapter. You may not have understood my point then. I hope you get it now. Being separated from God means fire, damnation, death, destruction, darkness, gloom, pain, hopelessness, and much, much more. But most of all, it means being alone.

I really hate to ask you to imagine yourself being separated from God. But just go there for a second.

What a horrific thought!

PART TWO

Being Found
Having an Awesome God Choose You

But because of his great love for us, God, who is rich in mercy, made us alive with Christ even when we were dead in transgressions—it is by grace you have been saved.
—EPHESIANS 2:4–5

I remember being chosen in the National Football League draft in 1992 by the Atlanta Falcons. Getting the call that they were selecting me was a moment that brought great jubilation to my life. I can also remember the agonizing moments of not being chosen as each round from first to seventh passed me by. Finally, I was chosen in the eighth round, and my life had direction.

There is nothing quite like hearing your name called when someone chooses you to be a part of something special. Imagine for a moment that on the first day of school, your teacher picks

only one student to get an A in the class. What if you were se-lected for this amazing deal? You have a 100 in the class, and you do not have to work for it. Everyone else will have to earn his grade. No way, right? It's too good to be true. Though it doesn't happen like that, it sure would be nice. God is not arbitrary like this teacher as He chooses who will be saved, but you have done no more to earn your salvation than this teacher required for you to earn an A. How awesome!

Keep walking with me and experience the greatest wonder of wonders. God who is rich in mercy and grace saw you and me just as we were and chose us to become members of His family. When God calls His eternal roll, listen intently . . . your name is next.

CHAPTER EIGHT

The Voice of God

When He Speaks, You'll Know It

"My sheep listen to my voice; I know them, and they follow me."
—JOHN 10:27

With certain voices in your life, no matter what you are doing, somehow you find a way to listen. Shhh, did you hear that? The voice of a mother who calls her child to dinner. The voice of a father who tells his children to stop arguing. The voice of a teacher who calls the roll. The voice of a coach who corrects a player. Recognizable voices that can't be mistaken for another, and when they speak, you listen. Though those voices are important, I want to tell you about the most significant voice you'll ever hear. I hope you are listening.

■　　■　　■

While playing in the National Football League, it was important for me to recognize the voice of the quarterback. As a running back, my every move depended upon what the commanding leader of the offense instructed. It was very important that I blocked out all other sounds and only tuned in to his voice. If you know anything about the game of football, you understand that in the heat of battle, particularly on an away game, there are many voices all around a player.

First, there are the voices of the fans that too often scream obscenities at the opposing team. I won't ever forget my introduction to professional football. In a preseason game back in 1992, my team, the Atlanta Falcons, went on the road to Cleveland. Never had I experienced such hostility by a crowd of people like the Browns fans. I'm not really mad at them. I actually wished they were rooting for me, because they gave their team an advantage with their noise. The Cleveland fans were the twelfth man on the field. Those Brown fans that day must have called us every ungodly thing you can possibly think of. OK . . . stop thinking. Let's concentrate on the good stuff. Their tactics didn't work. I think we won that game.

Second, coaches constantly yelled and screamed to make their point. "Stay wide on the toss!" or, "I told you to keep your head up so you can see the blitzing backer," or, "Get that ball up! Get that ball up! Keep the thing high and tight so you won't fumble." Up and down the sidelines they paced, giving every possible suggestion.

Last, but not least, who can forget the awful tactics of defensive players. They oftentimes tried to imitate the voice of my quarterback to throw me off. When that didn't work they called me names worse than the fans did. Defensive guys will do anything to get an edge.

In spite of all these many voices, I was taught to listen intently for the one voice that gave me the directions I needed while in the field of battle. When the quarterback spoke, I always recognized his voice and listened. OK, maybe if you pulled up some old film on me, you might spot one or two plays I botched up. But it wasn't my fault . . . it was the noise. Seriously though, when I responded to the quarterback's voice, I blocked the linebackers, faked out the defense, or ran for positive yardage. My point is I couldn't do my job until I heard the instructions from the right source.

■　　■　　■

During my sophomore year at Troy State University, I was involved in a ministry called Campus Outreach. I often attended a weekly campus meeting that was designed to help students develop in their relationship with God. At one particular meeting, staff member Calvin Cochran invited me to attend their summer beach project. The project was held in Fort Walton Beach, Florida.

The project's main purpose was to help college students experience ten weeks of intense spiritual training. I was a young believer, and I have to be honest, all that time with God sounded a little shaky to me. In addition to that, each student would be required to work a summer job. I needed money, but having to work all summer was not how I envisioned spending my summer days. The only appealing part to me at first was that the athletes who attended had opportunity to train and stay in shape for the upcoming year. I was very reluctant to go, but after several days of thinking it over and a lot of persuading by Calvin, I concluded that I would attend.

One of the ways in which God speaks to us is through other people. I really do believe that God was speaking to me through Calvin at that meeting to encourage me to go on the project. I needed to mature spiritually, and I needed guidance getting to that point. The Lord knew that, and He sent someone to get me where He wanted me to be.

After throwing a week's worth of clothes, a new toothbrush, one bottle of deodorant, four pairs of white tube socks, a set of swim trunks, my Bible, and a few other things into a garbage bag, I was all packed and ready to go.

When I arrived at the heavenly surroundings, I was there in body only. I was more concerned about my ability to stay in shape than I was about the purpose of the project. My focus on learning and growing in my relationship with Jesus Christ was secondary.

During the second week of the project, I experienced an unusual pain in my leg that prevented me from being able to work out. I couldn't run, lift weights, or even walk. I went to the doctor to get an examination, but nothing could be found that explained what was wrong with my leg. Every step I attempted put me in enormous pain.

I woke up the next morning, and the pain was miraculously gone. I had no idea what had happened. But I did know that somehow I was able to understand the purpose of the project. I truly believe that God spoke through my circumstance to get my attention. Before the leg injury, I was paying no attention to why God wanted me there. Needless to say, after He brought me through the injury, I paid attention so He'd never again have to use any cruel and unusual punishment to get my attention.

God's voice is like no other. It's not always an audible voice, like the time when He spoke at the baptism of Jesus (Matthew 3:16–17). Today He speaks mostly through Scripture. God also speaks through people and circumstances.

Found in Acts 16:22–30 is the story of Paul and Silas's imprisonment. The two were thrown into prison because they were practicing Christianity, which according to Roman law was not an approved religion. We are told that at about midnight Paul and Silas were praying and singing hymns of praises to God, and the prisoners were listening to them. I can picture myself in the jail, listening to the best sounds of a cappella harmony imaginable.

Suddenly there came a great earthquake that moved the very foundation of the prison. All the cell doors flung open, and everyone's chains sprang loose. When the jailer awoke and saw the prison doors opened, he drew his sword and was about to kill himself out of fear that the prisoners had escaped and he'd be killed as punishment for letting them escape. Paul then said with a loud voice, "Don't harm yourself! We are all here!" The guard was so amazed at what happened that he ran to Paul and Silas, fell at their feet, and asked, "What must I do to be saved?"

After Paul told him what to do, the jailer believed and was saved. Not only was he saved, but also everyone in his house believed and was saved. What a story of God speaking through people and circumstances! God spoke to the prison guard and his family through two jailed men. When God wants to get your attention, He can use anybody and anything.

■   ■   ■

When was the last time you heard the voice of God? Was He speaking through someone? Or was He speaking through some circumstance? Or did He speak through His Word, the Bible?

If you've never heard Him speak, you may want to read His Word. The apostle Paul in his letter to the Corinthian church says this in I Corinthians 15:1–4:

Now, brothers, I want to remind you of the gospel I preached to you, which you received and on which you have taken your stand. By this gospel you are saved, if you hold firmly to the word I preached to you. Otherwise, you have believed in vain. For what I received I passed on to you as of first importance: that Christ died for our sins according to the Scriptures, that he was buried, that he was raised on the third day according to the Scriptures.

God's Word is His mouthpiece of communication to you.

His voice is like no other. It's compelling. It gets your attention. It cares. It is calling. Hey, my friend, God is speaking. I hope you're listening. Scripture says, "Faith comes from hearing the message, and the message is heard through the word of Christ" (Romans 10:17). If you have heard God through faith, your life is now on the greatest road it can be on—the road that leads to heaven.

God's Gift of Grace

His Favor Toward Those He Loves

In order that in the coming ages he might show the incomparable riches of his grace, expressed in his kindness to us in Christ Jesus. For it is by grace you have been saved, through faith—and this not from yourselves, it is the gift of God.

—EPHESIANS 2:7–8

Do you like listening to pop, rock, country, R&B, or jazz? I like at least one song in all of those categories. My favorite music is Christian, or as some folks call it, gospel music. Actually, one of my favorite songs is one you've probably heard, "Amazing Grace." You know it. The first few lines say, "Amazing grace! how sweet the sound that saved a wretch like me! I once was lost, but now am found. Was blind, but now I see."

That song speaks to my heart. Every time I hear the words spoken without music, every time I sing it (or try to sing it, because I don't have that great a voice), and every time I hear it sung in any style, I feel blessed. The lyrics are clearly talking about me. I was a sinner and could do nothing to deserve God's love. Despite me, He sent His Son to save my soul. What grace!

Think for a moment about the last time you were given

something special that you didn't deserve. Maybe you got money from your parents, even though your report card was horrible. Or it could have been forgiveness by your best friend when you hurt him or her. Or it might have been an extra chance by a kind professor to let you retake a test you failed, or a warning rather than a speeding ticket. Well, that's called grace. There was nothing you did to earn it. You didn't deserve it. You needed a break. You were in need and somehow the need was met.

There is another way I love to describe grace. The best example of grace is what God did through Jesus Christ on the cross —an undeserved favor or gift given to you though you didn't deserve it. Jesus was nailed to a wooden cross to demonstrate His love for all humanity. He experienced a slow suffocating death called the crucifixion. And He experienced it just for you. The cross was not only a painful experience, but according to Roman law the crucifixion was a place of shame. Jesus took the shame that was meant for you and me and put it upon Himself. My friend, that's called grace.

■ ■ ■

My time at Troy State came to an unexpected halt. I found out that my junior year on the football team was actually my senior year. The program was moving from Division II status to Division IAA status, which would give me too many semester hours to continue my NCAA college football career.

I had completed nine semesters at Troy State at the closing of the fall football season. Due to the fact that Troy State moved its program up to Division IAA, I still had one semester of eligibility left. However, I could only complete it at a NAIA school. Division II football players are allowed ten semesters to complete their eligibility. And with only one semester of eligibility remaining, I had to sit out the second semester of that academic year. This would allow me to save my final semester for the fall. Now if all that's confusing, I understand. The NCAA rules have been known to confuse the brightest of minds.

At the end of the fall semester, I attended a Campus Outreach Christmas conference. The conference was held in Gatlinburg, Tennessee, and it was for college students from all around the country who wanted to grow in their faith. The speakers were awesome, and the breakout seminars were enlightening.

One of the seminar teachers was named Steve Shadrach. Steve and his wife were from Conway, Arkansas. He was the founder of an organization called Student Mobilization. I would later come to understand why meeting Steve was so important for me. The conference came to an end, and I made my way home to Albany, Georgia. While at home, I was contacted by my coaches from Troy State. I was told I could possibly attend the University of Central Arkansas to complete my eligibility. The school was located in Conway. You noticed—that's the same place Steve Shadrach was from. Without a dime in my pocket and with only an old beat-up suitcase, I made my way to Arkansas.

I was unable to enroll the second semester because I had only one semester of eligibility remaining. Central Arkansas had a conference rule that stated that I had to be a resident for sixteen weeks in order to participate in the fall. I was trapped between a rock and a hard place. If I enrolled in the winter, I would have no more semesters remaining to play in the fall. But if I didn't enroll, I would not meet the sixteen weeks' residency rule.

Disappointed, of course, I left Arkansas for home, and I didn't know what I was going to do with my life. After being home for two days, I was about to start a job at a local restaurant.

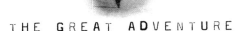

The night before I was to start, I got a phone call from Steve Shadrach. He heard about what had happened to me and asked me if I'd like to move to Conway to live with him and his family. Naturally I said, "For what?" He said he was really impressed with meeting me at the Christmas conference and that he felt led to call and see how he could help me. You have to understand, I had only spoken to Steve for a few hours at that conference. After talking it over with my mom, I accepted his invitation and moved in with him and his family. I lived there for six months. Finally I ended up at Northeastern State University in Oklahoma for the fall. The University of Central Arkansas coaches found a school where the sixteen-week residency rule did not apply.

My time with Steve and his family was a turning point in my life. It was one of the greatest experiences of grace I have ever had. They fed me and housed me. What was theirs was mine. I wasn't part of their family, and I didn't deserve such treatment, but I received it.

■   ■   ■

One of my favorite Bible stories that communicates what grace is all about is the story of the Prodigal Son, from Luke 15:11–31. This passage tells about a father who had two sons who would inherit shares of his estate.

For a long while, the sons loved living on the land. I would have loved it as well. Living with the father who loved me. Eating the best of foods and living in a secure place. Well, the younger son didn't agree with me. Seems he grew tired of the good life. Go figure, right?

The younger of the two sons demanded cash for his share of the property, left town, and spent his wealth on wild living and doing what he wanted. I imagine the partying was good for a while. No rules, just fun. He probably was the life of the party, because I imagine he paid the bill for everyone who attended. After spending all of his wealth, he found himself lower than he'd ever been in his life. He had to eat pig slop with the pigs. Yuck!

He finally came to his senses and decided to go home to be a servant for his father. However, his father was so moved at seeing his son return home that he prepared the greatest feast for him. He held nothing against his son. Instead, he forgave him and showed grace toward him.

> But the father said to his servants, "Quick! Bring the best robe and put it on him. Put a ring on his finger and sandals on his feet. Bring the fattened calf and kill it. Let's have a feast and celebrate. For this son of mine was dead and is alive again; he was lost and is found." So they began to celebrate. (Luke 15:22–24)

This is true grace. What a person doesn't deserve is freely given to him. The son even planned to earn his way back by working as one of his father's hired men. But grace is not what you do; it is what someone does on your behalf, though you don't deserve it.

Again, grace is what God the Father gives. You can't earn your way back to God. He freely receives you through repentance of sin. Since God has favor toward His creation even though it has fallen into sin, He desires to be in fellowship with that creation.

The Bible is comprised of sixty-six books, thirty-nine in the Old Testament and twenty-seven in the New Testament. Authors were inspired by God to write these wonderful stories, all stories of grace. God did through Jesus Christ what we could not do for ourselves.

Romans 5:20–21 (NASB) says, "The Law came in so that

the transgression would increase; but where sin increased, grace abounded all the more, so that, as sin reigned in death, even so grace might reign through righteousness to eternal life through Jesus Christ our Lord." Think about your life. Think about where you were. Think about where you are. Think about whose you are. Think about the love the heavenly Father has for you. Even after all that, even if you fall, God's grace will still be there to pick you up. Isn't His grace truly amazing?

CHAPTER TEN

Ears That Hear

Listen, He's Calling

My sheep listen to my voice; I know them, and they follow me.

—JOHN 10:27

You may know the ears I'm talking about in the title to this chapter. I'm not talking about the ears that are attached to your head. I'm talking about the ears that are attached to your heart. Only those who have had their spiritual ears opened can hear the voice of God.

■　　■　　■

I had a friend named Jeff who told me of his newfound desire for God. He had been attending church services on a pretty consistent basis for about five weeks. One particular week the pastor was teaching on the love of God. Unlike any other moment before, Jeff said that he could hear the message as clear as he could the music playing on his brand new entertainment system. Jeff understood, accepted, and received the Word.

He could not believe that God could love him and the world as much as He does—enough that He would give His only Son, Jesus Christ. The message moved him so much that when the pastor gave the invitation to come and receive Jesus Christ, Jeff got up and walked to the altar and prayed the sinner's prayer. In his heart he could hear the voice of God calling him into a relationship. It is the heart that matters the most with God. Therefore it is with the heart that we hear the voice of God, not with the ears.

■　　■　　■

I often attended a campus meeting with the ministry of Campus Outreach. It was an opportunity for students to grow and worship God and fellowship with others. During one meeting, unlike anytime before, I heard the voice of God, speaking through many different believers.

One student gave a testimony of what God did for him on a summer project. Another talked about how God deepened his passion for world evangelism. Yet another spoke of how God helped her with confidence to share her faith.

For the first time, I wanted to deepen my relationship with God. My desire for God and His people grew and developed. The ears of my heart were open and I could hear the voice of God.

■　　■　　■

One of my favorite parables in the Bible is the parable of the sower, found in Matthew 13:3–23. The parable is unique because

Jesus interpreted its meaning, something He seldom did. He gave us four accounts of the kind of person who hears the Word.

First there's the one who hears the Word and does not understand it. Ever sit in class and hear the professor lecture on a particular subject and not understand it? Ever hear a sermon preached, and at the end of the sermon you realize you didn't understand a word of it? Ever visit a foreign country and not understand most of the words spoken? This is the state of the person on whom seed was sown beside the road. He hears the Word, but doesn't understand it.

The second account is that of the man who hears the Word and immediately receives it with joy; yet he has no firm root in the Word. His temporary interest in the Bible or Christianity is weak, and when affliction or persecution arrives because of the Word, immediately he loses interest. Sometimes when things get difficult, what we discover is that we have no root system in place to endure the difficult time. This is the one on whom seed was sown in rocky places.

Next is the man who hears the Word, but the worry of the world and the deceitfulness of wealth choke the Word and it becomes unfruitful. It is so easy for the things of this life to become your focus: education, sports, or even your desires to be rich. "For the love of money is a root of all kinds of evil. Some people, eager for money, have wandered from the faith and pierced themselves with many griefs" (I Timothy 6:10). Wealth promises happiness and fulfillment, but when the end comes, it can't deliver you from your sin or from emptiness. These are the people on whom the seed was sown among the thorns.

Finally, there is the man who hears the Word and understands it. This person bears fruit by telling others about Jesus—for some the fruit is a hundredfold, some sixty, and some thirty.

These are the ones who hear the Word and the voice of God and actually act on it and bring forth fruit. These hearers hear with their hearts and not with their ears.

Are the ears of your heart open to the voice of God? Do you hear the voice of God calling? If your ears are open and you hear the voice of God, you will then desire to live for God and do the things God desires. The people you want to spend your time with will change. The places you went that were not of God, you won't want to go to anymore. Your passions will become godly passions. Your view of people and sin will change. Second Corinthians 5:17 says, "Therefore, if anyone is in Christ, he is a new creation; the old has gone, the new has come!"

Have you heard the voice of God lately? Can you hear Him calling? If so, you won't remain the same. The voice of God is the sweetest sound you'll hear.

CHAPTER ELEVEN

Eyes That See

No Longer Blind to the Truth

Open my eyes that I may see wonderful things in your law.
—PSALM 119:18

One of the greatest gifts that God has given is the gift of sight. To be able to see the beauty of a sunset, or the wonder of the Grand Canyon, or even the stars in a beautiful night's sky is truly wonderful. But it's not nearly as wonderful as having spiritual sight. To have spiritual sight is the greatest gift there is—having once been blind to the truth about God and now being able to see.

I remember when I first heard the biblical truth about God. It was like being able to see for the first time. Of course I grew up hearing about Him, but never had I heard, in such biblical detail, the things that He did for me. I was told that God gave His only begotten Son, Jesus Christ, to die on the cross for my sins. I was told that Christ was buried and was raised from the dead to give me life. I also was told that if I placed my faith in Christ, I would be saved from an eternal death that would separate me from God forever. After hearing these incredible truths about God, I wanted to know Him, and I wanted to make Him known. I found myself telling my friends how I had come to know who God is. The scales were removed from my eyes, and I had vision.

I remember during my college years the days of going to class and trying to learn a difficult subject. I would attempt to understand it, but I continued to struggle. It was difficult to see how things were supposed to be. Finally, after hearing it over and over, it began to make sense. One thing would make sense, then another and another, until finally I got it and that particular subject had a whole new meaning. I was no longer blind to the truth. Something opened my eyes, and now I could see. I began to find success in class as I understood the subject. I had new confidence, and the class had meaning.

Jesus performed many miracles for one purpose: so that people would no longer be blind to the truth that He is the Son of God. John 9 tells us of a blind beggar who had an encounter with Jesus. Jesus saw the blind man while passing by, and His disciples asked Him whose sin was the reason for this man's blindness. Jesus told His disciples that it was neither the man who had sinned nor his parents, but he was born blind so that the work of God would be displayed in his life. The Bible goes on to tell us that Jesus spat on the ground, made clay from His saliva, and applied it to the eyes of the blind man. Jesus then told the blind beggar to wash his eyes in the nearby pool of water. After doing this, the man's sight arrived.

Jesus is the only one who causes the blind to see. The Jews were so upset with what had happened that they had the man put out of the synagogue (John 9:34). Verse 38 tells us that this blind man who was given sight was found by Jesus, and he said, "Lord, I believe." Not only did Jesus come to heal the physically blind, but He also came to heal the spiritually blind. Jesus says, "For judgment I have come into this world, so that the blind will see and that those who see will become blind" (John 9:39).

The world is filled with distractions and material things that keep us from seeing the truth about God. Second Corinthians 4:3–4 says, "And even if our gospel is veiled, it is veiled to those who are perishing. The god of this age has blinded the minds of unbelievers, so that they cannot see the light of the gospel of the glory of Christ, who is the image of God." Satan has turned men and women away with lesser ambitions and desires that are not eternal. For you, it may be your education or your athletic team. It may be your boyfriend or girlfriend. Maybe your greatest dream is to make a lot of money and live like the rich and famous.

Oh, how easy it is to live on a college campus for four years, or to go to work day after day, groping around in the dark of academics, athletics, and a social life and never see the light. Psalm 119:18 says, "Open my eyes that I may see wonderful things in your law." God is the only one who gives sight to the spiritually blind. He opens the eyes of those who are groping around in spiritual darkness and gives them sight, the sight to see the wonderful things about God and His Son Jesus Christ.

It is the truth that Jesus was born of a virgin and lived a sinless life. It is the truth that He was crucified on the cross for the sins of the world, was placed in a tomb, and on the third day arose from the dead. It is the truth that those who place their faith in Him will live eternally with Him after they pass from this life.

When Christ gives you sight, you are no longer blind to the truth. Do you have your facts together? Do you see the truth of who Jesus really is? Have you been told that He makes blind men see? You just have. Now open your eyes.

CHAPTER TWELVE

Made Alive

We've Been Given New Life

Therefore, if anyone is in Christ, he is a new creation; the old has gone, the new has come!

—2 CORINTHIANS 5:17

There's something about having something new that puts a smile on your face. It puts pep in your step and a glide in your slide. I remember my mom buying me new shoes from time to time. Brand-new, spot free, dirt free, and cool. You have to understand that in the neighborhood where I grew up, new shoes meant that a kid could outrun anybody in the neighborhood. It was all in the shoes.

What was so cool was that everyone recognized that I was wearing new shoes. "Hey, Derrick's got on new shoes." "Where did you get those from?" "How much did they cost?" When the day was over, I took them off, cleaned them up, and put them away in a nice safe place. I couldn't wait until the next morning so that I could put them back on. I rejoiced that they were mine, and I wanted everyone to know that they were mine.

Well, maybe it wasn't new shoes for you. Maybe it was that new car that your parents purchased for you to drive to college, or maybe it was your new computer so that you could be more efficient with your work. Whatever it was, the fact that it was new and that it was yours changed your world.

All summer, Tiffany drove an old 1996 Paseo. She had just finished her senior year in high school and was ready for college. One problem: Her car had two hundred and twenty-five thousand miles on it, and it began to have some major engine problems.

Her parents had invested hundreds of dollars trying to repair the car, but it continued to give her problems. Finally, they realized that it wasn't worth it to continue pouring money into a car that continued to have one problem after another. Her parents knew that she was going a long way from home for college, and they wanted her to have something more reliable. To her surprise, her parents purchased her a brand-new, four door Honda Accord. It was fully loaded with a CD changer, a retractable sunroof, and heated seats. What more could she want?

Tiffany made her way home from work in her usual fashion, driving her old worn-out Paseo. When she arrived in her driveway, she saw a car that was completely unfamiliar. She thought that the car belonged to one of her parents' friends. She made her way into the house, only to find that there was no one inside except her mother and father.

She then asked the obvious question, "Whose car is that in the driveway?"

Her parents paused for a second, smiled, and then said, "It's yours."

"Mine," she replied, "what do you mean it's mine?"

"It's yours," they said again.

Finally, it registered that her parents had just bought her a brand-new car. She screamed at the top of her lungs and ran out the door. The neighbors came out, wondering what was going on. She began to tell everyone that she had just been given a new car for college. Her parents told her that they wanted her to have the peace of mind that her car would be able to handle the long drive to school. There's nothing like being given something new.

The Bible tells us in 2 Corinthians 5:17 that those of us who are in Jesus Christ have been given new life. We were once dead in our sins, and now we've been made alive in Him. "If anyone is in Christ, he is a new creation; the old has gone, the new has come!" You and I have been made alive through the death and resurrection of Jesus Christ. Those who are in Christ are alive. Though we were once dead in our sins through the death of Adam and his sin, we now have been made alive through the power of the resurrection of Jesus Christ. The old life is no more. The new life has come. No longer do you have to live the way you used to live. You don't have to go to the places that you used to go. You don't have to talk the way you used to talk. You are no longer the same person. Outwardly you may still look the same, but inwardly you have been made alive.

Nothing quite captures this marvelous truth like Matthew 9:17, where Jesus answered a question from John's disciples as to why His disciples weren't fasting. First He told them that His disciples weren't fasting yet because He was still with them, and no one fasts while a wedding reception is still going on. Jesus then told them that no one puts new wine into old wineskins; otherwise the wineskins burst, the wine pours out, and the wineskins are ruined; but if they put new wine into fresh wineskins, both are preserved.

When you become new in Christ, the old lifestyle doesn't fit into the new life that God brings when He makes you alive in Jesus Christ. Jesus brings newness that can't be confined within the old forms. What you become in Christ doesn't mix with the old person you used to be. You are alive because Jesus is alive in you. The next time you are tempted to go to the old places, just remember you can't put new wine into old wineskins. Believe me, the wineskins won't hold.

CHAPTER THIRTEEN

The Greatest Gift

Thank God for Salvation

But the gift of God is eternal life in Christ Jesus our Lord.

—ROMANS 6:23

A gift is something given to you freely by another. You might not have known it was coming. You didn't expect it. You simply received it and walked away thankful. As far back as I can remember, opening birthday presents was one of the most exciting times of my life. All of those presents and gifts just for me. My moment in the sun. It seemed that on my birthday I was given more gifts than I knew what to do with. I loved opening each gift, tearing open the box and seeing what was in the package. Do you remember those moments? How did it make you feel? Important? Thankful? Well, for me, I felt like the most special person on the planet.

I remember in my sophomore year of college, my roommate's parents surprised him one Saturday morning and gave him what he thought was the greatest gift he could ever receive. It was a brand-new black T-top Camaro with all the bells and whistles. The sunroof was electronically powered. It had a CD player and cassette player. The seats were all powered, and the interior was all leather. One minute he was walking, and the next he was riding.

It's amazing how things can change so quickly. Everyone on campus knew he had a new car. Now me, being his roommate and all, of course I was the first to ride in it. You talk about smooth. It was as if we were floating down the road. Every weekend he would wash and wax his new car. He would detail the interior and exterior. The tires and rims were so shiny that you had to wear sunglasses to look at them. What a gift! He was so thankful to his parents for providing him with that new car. It was totally unexpected.

As I look back to that experience, I must confess that it certainly did appear to be the greatest gift one could receive. Can you imagine it? A college student in his sophomore year was driving a brand-new Camaro. What a great gift.

During our junior year in college, my roommate became a Christian. He discussed with me what the gift of salvation meant to him. He said, "No question, no gift in the world can compare to the gift of salvation. God freely gave Jesus Christ, His only Son, as a gift to me, to bring me salvation. My life has new meaning, purpose, and direction. I now know what is most important in life and what is least important. My Camaro was a great gift, but it wasn't the greatest gift. My salvation through Jesus Christ was the greatest gift I have ever received, and nothing else compares to it."

Luke 2 records the miraculous birth of the Lord Jesus Christ, the one who would be declared Savior of the world. A census was sent out to all the Roman world by Caesar Augustus; all the people had to register for the census. Joseph and Mary, who were engaged to be married, made their way to the census. While there, Mary gave birth to her firstborn son. She wrapped Him in cloth and laid Him in the manger. The inn was completely full, and there was no place for Mary and the baby to rest. Shepherds were visited by an angel who declared to them that a Savior had been born, who is Christ the Lord. He is God's gift to the world, and each Christmas we celebrate the wonderful, magnificent birth of Jesus Christ. He is the real reason for the season.

"For to us a child is born, to us a son is given, and the government will be on his shoulders. And he will be called Wonderful Counselor, Mighty God, Everlasting Father, Prince of Peace" (Isaiah 9:6).

The next time you open your Christmas presents, be sure to open the one that says, "From God . . . to you." You'll be glad you did.

CHAPTER FOURTEEN

Nothing to Boast About

All Credit Given to God

But as it is, you boast in your arrogance; all such boasting is evil.

—JAMES 4:16 (NASB)

In a society that brags and says, "Look at what I've done; it's because of me that I have the things I have," I would imagine that you spend days listening to people boast about their accomplishments, how excellent they are at academics and athletics. "I've made the dean's list the last three consecutive semesters. Bet you don't know anyone who's done that before." "Did you see the way that I dribbled the ball between my legs, crossed my defender over, and pulled up for the J?" "Nobody's got game like me." Thank goodness that no one can boast about his or her salvation. Salvation is not the work of man on earth, but the work of Jesus Christ on the cross. It is not what you do. It is what He has done.

> Surely he took up our infirmities and carried our sorrows, yet we considered him stricken by God, smitten by him, and afflicted.

But he was pierced for our transgressions, he was crushed for our iniquities; the punishment that brought us peace was upon him, and by his wounds we are healed. (Isaiah 53:4–5)

I had the wonderful privilege of playing professional football for six years. The greatest player I ever had the opportunity of playing with was Barry Sanders, running back for the Detroit Lions. I've never seen anyone who compares to Barry Sanders as a football player. He is legendary for his ability to change direction while moving full speed. A coach once said that trying to tackle Barry was like trying to catch a chicken in the yard. Just when you think you've got him cornered, he changes directions.

I can't ever remember Barry boasting or bragging about his ability. Never once did he say, "Look at me," or, "Look at what I've done." In one particular game against Atlanta I saw him make a run that just defied logic. He took the ball while running wide right. It seemed like seven or eight guys had him trapped with nowhere to go, but in Barry-like fashion, he changed directions, came back to the left, and scored from thirty-five yards out.

No one else on earth could have made that run but Barry. After the game, I said to him, "How in the world did you get out of that situation and score from thirty-five yards away?" He looked at me and said, "Derrick, God gave me that." From that day forward he became one of my heroes.

The Bible says, "Every good and perfect gift is from above, coming down from the Father of the heavenly lights, who does not change like shifting shadows" (James 1:17).

I had a friend in college who truly believed that his salvation was completely dependent upon his own work and good deeds. He believed that if he prayed enough or went to church enough, it would earn him favor from God and thus make him acceptable in the sight of God. It wasn't until I had the chance to talk with him one spring semester that he really came to understand that salvation and a relationship with Jesus Christ were not dependent upon what he did, but instead were based on what Jesus did on the cross.

The passage I discussed with him was Ephesians 2:8–9, "For by grace you have been saved through faith; and that not of yourselves, it is the gift of God; not as a result of works, so that no one may boast" (NASB). I remember him saying in response to me, "You mean that it's nothing that I've done, but what He's done?" With a look of amazement on his face, he simply said, "Wow!"

The apostle Paul gives us an account of what God through Jesus Christ did on the cross to justify the believer. The word *justify* means to vindicate or free someone. Romans 3:23–27 says:

> For all have sinned and fall short of the glory of God, and are justified freely by his grace though the redemption that came by Christ Jesus. God presented him as a sacrifice of atonement, through faith in his blood. He did this to demonstrate his justice, because in his forbearance he had left the sins committed beforehand unpunished—he did it to demonstrate his justice at the present time, so as to be just and the one who justifies those who have faith in Jesus. Where, then, is boasting? It is excluded.

God deserves all of the glory for your salvation through Jesus Christ. Without Christ there is no salvation. What you have in salvation is all God's doing. Every bit of it.

PART THREE

Shown the Way
Learning How to Live the Christian Life

For we are God's workmanship, created in Christ Jesus to do good works, which God prepared in advance for us to do.
—EPHESIANS 2:10

The first day at a new school, how do you find your way around? When you're taking up a new sport, how do you learn the game? When you start a new job, how do you learn what to do? Well, usually someone shows you the way.

Such is the case in the life of someone who has entered into a relationship with Jesus Christ. Through the person of the Holy Spirit, He guides you and directs your life for the purpose of making God look good. Psalm 119:18 says, "Open my eyes that I may see wonderful things in your law." The persons of the Trinity are God represented in three dimensions: God the Father, God the Son (Jesus Christ), and God the Holy Spirit. They are all working together to illuminate the Bible for you and show you the way to live the Christian life.

Therefore, you don't have to walk the campus unassisted in your effort to find the class. You have help to teach you how to live the Christian life. There is a guide who comes alongside of you and walks you to the door. Welcome to class. Did you notice who the teacher is? It is God Himself.

CHAPTER FIFTEEN

The Person Inside

The Incredible Work of the Holy Spirit

I will ask the Father, and he will give you another Counselor to be with you forever.

—JOHN 14:16

I don't believe anyone can quite put into words the incredible love a mother has for her children. She loves you when you are right, and she loves you when you are wrong. Not that she condones your wrong, but she still loves you. The work of a mom is without end, and her love has no competition. When things don't work out the way we hope, she's there to provide comfort. When we seem to lose our way, she's like a compass that guides and gives us directions. Moms seem to be there through all of life's experiences, whether good or bad. They are faithful and tireless in their efforts to nurture and help the children they love in any way possible. The love and commitment of a mother never changes. Now that I am all grown up, I thought my mom's view of me would change. It hasn't. She still thinks I'm her baby.

To be perfectly honest, when I see her or talk to her, I still like to act like I am her baby. Hey, don't laugh at me—I bet you do too.

■   ■   ■

During my first year in the National Football League, I had what was probably the hardest training camp I have ever experienced in my life. I was an eighth round draft pick, and my chances of making the team were slim and almost none. Every day my body was being put to the test, and my mind was being stretched like never before. All I wanted was for someone to help me get through that difficult time. Every single day I wanted to talk to my mom over the phone. She was always there to hear me talk about my experiences in camp.

I would tell her about the difficult early morning practices, which seemed to be the more physical practices of the two that were scheduled. I shared with her how the evening meetings seemed as if they would never end. Finally, the mental anguish of just trying to make the team was unlike anything I had ever encountered, and I told her about that.

For four weeks, my mom comforted me and encouraged me through every moment of that experience. I really believe that her constant presence helped me endure training camp. In case you were wondering, I made the team. Thanks, Mom!

■   ■   ■

God the Father has provided you and me the help we need to accomplish all that He desires of us. The Holy Spirit lives inside those of us who have placed our faith in Christ, and He is our help. He is a real person. He is alive and actively participating in the affairs of those who believe in Jesus Christ. Jesus said, when He explained the coming of the Holy Spirit, "I will ask the Father, and he will give you another Counselor to be with you forever—the Spirit of truth. The world cannot accept him, because it neither sees him nor knows him. But you know him, for he lives with you and will be in you" (John 14:16–17).

The power to be successful in the Christian life has been provided through the person of the Holy Spirit. Jesus said in Luke 24:49, "I am going to send you what my Father has promised; but stay in the city until you have been clothed with power from on high." Acts 2 fulfilled this promise when the Holy Spirit actually arrived. Because of His presence in the Christian's life, we now have within us the power and supernatural help we need to be victorious. He is a comforter, a helper, a companion, and a friend. His work is endless, His effort is tireless, and His love is unconditional. No one works for you like the person of the Holy Spirit does. He is also the third person of the Trinity (God the Father, God the Son, and God the Holy Spirit).

Perhaps you're thinking: *God actually lives inside of me?* Yes, He does, if you're a believer, through the person of the Holy Spirit. In a world filled with challenges, obstacles, and temptations, you have been given a guide to help you find your way through this maze we call life.

As a little boy, I used to be afraid of the dark. I would cry for my mom to come sit with me until I fell asleep. She always did. She was committed, faithful, and always present. What a comfort! You don't have to fear the darkness of this world. The person of the Holy Spirit has come to keep you company. Isn't it great to know you have help?

CHAPTER SIXTEEN

His Workmanship
God's Very Own Masterpiece

For we are God's workmanship, created in Christ Jesus to do good works, which God prepared in advance for us to do.

—EPHESIANS 2:10

Have you ever thought that the day your parents sent you away for college you would be representing some eighteen years of their investment in you? From the time you were born, you have become the masterpiece that your parents have developed over the years. You are their work of art, and it is their desire to see you bring forth the kind of good works that tell others they have done a good job.

Can't you hear them talking? "This is my son or daughter whom I am presenting to you as my masterpiece. My work of art for eighteen years. He/she is presented to you with ethics, integrity, character, and gifts and skills." It's time to represent them well.

■　　■　　■

My road to Troy State University was unconventional to say the least. I didn't get the scholarship I had hoped for after leaving high school. So I decided to attend a junior college for a year to reassess what road would be the most advantageous. My desire was to graduate from college with a degree and to possibly get an opportunity to play professional football.

My mom was my greatest encourager in holding me accountable for making the best grades I could. Every day she asked me how things were going in the classroom. She often said, "Give yourself options by getting a college education."

I also had a very good friend who was a personal trainer. For an entire year, he invested all of his expertise in helping me develop my athletic skill. In a year's time I went from weighing 195 pounds to weighing 225 pounds. As I started the year, I ran the forty-yard dash in 4.58 seconds. In a year's time I could run it in 4.36 seconds. Every aspect of my physical profile improved. I was now ready to move on to a four-year institution.

The day I arrived at Troy State University, I believed that I was not only representing myself, but also those who had invested so much in developing me into the person I had become. I was their work of art. I was their masterpiece. My success was their success.

There is nothing like the grades that come out the first semester at college. Your parents are looking forward to seeing A's and B's. Hopefully that's what you deliver. They can't wait to tell their friends and coworkers how good you are doing in school.

But the ultimate crowning moment of your college experience will be the day you graduate. You can't fully comprehend the joy your parents will experience when this moment takes place. For one, they won't have to write any more checks to pay your tuition. Finally the crowning moment arrives. There you are in your cap and gown. There they are with smiles that say, "Job well done!" Cameras are flashing, capturing the moment. You are on one of life's grandest stages receiving your degree and making your parents look good.

Much like that, your life mission is to make God look good. The way God looks good in you is by your doing that which glorifies Him.

■   ■   ■

Ephesians 2:10 says, "For we are God's workmanship, created in Christ Jesus to do good works, which God prepared in advance for us to do."

The things you say, the places you go, and the things you do should represent Christ in you. Found in Matthew 28:18–20 is what we call the Great Commission. Jesus had invested the better part of three and a half years with the disciples, pouring His life into theirs and teaching them how to fish for men. Everything that they did represented what Christ had done in them.

All authority in heaven and on earth has been given to me. Therefore go and make disciples of all nations, baptizing them in the name of the Father and of the Son and of the Holy Spirit, and teaching them to obey everything I have commanded you. And surely I am with you always, to the very end of the age. (Matthew 28:18–20)

His workmanship was created for good works.

■   ■   ■

You are now God's masterpiece, His workmanship. His work of art. God wants to present you to the lost so that through you He might reveal Himself to others. God really enjoys showing you off.

CHAPTER SEVENTEEN

Going to Worship

Why Church Is Important

If I am delayed, you will know how people ought to conduct themselves in God's household, which is the church of the living God, the pillar and foundation of the truth.

—1 TIMOTHY 3:15

While growing up, going to church was probably something you just did. You didn't have to know why you did it. You were told to go, and you went. No questions asked. Most students I talk with had the same experience. Some even tell of how they went to church two or three times a week. Monday night choir practice, youth group, Wednesday night Bible study, Sunday morning worship, and sometimes Sunday evening worship. Maybe this is why some college students agonize over going to church on Sunday morning. You know what I'm talking about. By the time you reach college, you may feel all churched out.

Well, I must confess, I don't believe a person can get enough of going to church. When I was a kid, it seemed that I was in church every day, although I didn't always know why. I couldn't wait to leave home for college so that I could make my own decision about going to church. If some of you are honest, you have felt the same way. It wasn't until I surrendered my life to Jesus Christ and came to know Him in a personal relationship that this thing called going to church made sense.

I learned that a person could be in church and not be in Christ. For a long time I was in church but not in Christ; therefore, church was only a place to go and fill some religious void. It wasn't until I experienced Jesus Christ that it became a place that satisfied my appetite for God. "If anyone is in Christ, he is a new creation; the old has gone, the new has come!" (2 Corinthians 5:17).

After receiving Christ, church was no longer some boring duty or obligation. I now attend church to be a part of the assembly of those who believe in the Lord Jesus Christ; I desire to be around the people of God. During my freshman year of college, my roommate and I attended church on a pretty regular basis. Each Sunday we would get up, get dressed, and off we went. Sometimes we even invited other students to go with us.

Of course, Sunday morning comes after Saturday night. Most students find it easier to sleep in on Sunday morning than to get up and attend a church service. I believe what kept me in on Saturday night also got me up on Sunday morning. What kept me in was Jesus Christ living on the inside of my heart. Staying in is tough, and getting up even tougher, if you don't have a personal relationship with Christ.

I knew that I would be inspired by a message from the pastor. I also knew that the church would pray for me. In days like these, you had better have someone praying for and with you. In totality, church gave me a complete sense of peace.

One Sunday morning in my college years, I invited a friend from my dorm to attend a service with me. He wasn't very inclined to go, but because of our friendship he decided to come. He was in his sophomore year and had not attended church for the two years he had been on campus. After attending the service, he told me he really enjoyed going. He then initiated going the next week. At this particular service, he prayed to receive Jesus Christ as his Lord and Savior. The one person he didn't plan to meet, he met. His entire life changed.

Jesus placed a tremendous emphasis on the church. In His passion for proper worship within God's house (which was the temple at that point), Jesus saw that some were selling animals for unfair prices within the confines of the temple court. So Jesus, in a moment of righteous anger, made it very clear what the purpose of the church was. "'It is written,' he said to them, "'My house will be a house of prayer"; but you have made it "a den of robbers"'" (Luke 19:45–46).

The church is a place to worship God and assemble and fellowship with one another so that God might be glorified.

Let us hold unswervingly to the hope we profess, for he who promised is faithful. And let us consider how we may spur one another on toward love and good deeds. Let us not give up meeting together, as some are in the habit of doing, but let us encourage one another—and all the more as you see the Day approaching. (Hebrews 10:23–25)

Oh yeah, let me give you an update on my college friend. Saturday night became a distant memory, and Sunday morning became a way of life. You see, the party was no longer in the fraternity house but in the church house. He no longer drinks from the bottle that brings death; he now drinks from the bottle that brings life. He no longer follows the crowd; he now follows the Savior.

Well, my goodness, what do you know—it's almost Sunday. Want to go to church?

CHAPTER EIGHTEEN

A Disciple of Christ

How to Live by the Commands of Christ

All authority in heaven and on earth has been given to me. Therefore go and make disciples of all nations, baptizing them in the name of the Father and of the Son and of the Holy Spirit, and teaching them to obey everything I have commanded you. And surely I am with you always, to the very end of the age.

—MATTHEW 28:19–20

Boy, don't I know how hard it is to do what someone else wants you to do. Or what about going somewhere someone wants you to go? Or even simply saying what someone wants you to say? This can certainly be challenging. Before entering college, I had no idea what a disciple for Christ was. I didn't even know what a disciple was. I thought that once I gave my life to Jesus by accepting Him into my heart, I had done enough. I learned quickly that a mere confession of Christ was only the beginning of what was called a relationship with Christ. I slowly began to understand that God wanted me to follow Him daily as a way of life that brings glory to His name.

This idea of following Jesus was totally foreign to me. All I knew was that I was a Christian, and, if I went to church every Sunday, I would be experiencing a relationship with God. As time progressed, I learned that being a Christian is far more than just church attendance on Sunday. It meant giving myself to Christ and following Him on a daily basis.

I was introduced to what I now believe to be one of the greatest Bible verses on the subject of being a disciple of Christ. Jesus says in Matthew 16:24, "If anyone would come after me, he must deny himself and take up his cross and follow me." Hearing this passage was like a whack between the eyes. I guess it made me sense that if I was going to follow Jesus, I had to deny myself the things I wanted for the things He wanted. I got involved in a small discipleship group on campus that really helped me learn more than just the surface meaning of the Scriptures.

I was able, through training, to unfold an even deeper meaning of God's Word. What amazed me the most was the confidence and boldness I gained to articulate my faith in Christ. While on campus, there were numerous opportunities to share Christ with others. Every day I would wake up and attempt to convince myself to share my faith with someone that day. But in the very early stages of being pulled into the ministry on campus, I didn't have the confidence to do so. After spending time in a small discipleship group, my faith and confidence soared. All that I didn't have, I finally had after gaining the necessary training that was so critical in my growth. It was one of the single most significant reasons I was able to grow in my faith and develop a desire to follow Christ. When I accepted Christ, I also accepted the call to discipleship. It's the entire package, not part of it.

■ ■ ■

God's intentions for the Christian are for him or her to live each and every day according to His commands. You don't have to give in to the pressures of college life. You can live far beyond the sex and alcohol and drugs and cheating that plague so many students. I know that these are all real temptations and struggles for students. Believe it or not, I also know that these can be struggles for Christians as well. No one is exempt from the wiles of the Enemy.

One particular Christian student told me how he had begun to struggle with looking with wrong intentions at the girls. Every day was a struggle, and he didn't feel as though he had any answers. After spending some time with him, I discovered that he had no really structured way of getting time with God. He wasn't spending any time in God's Word. He had no prayer life, nor was he surrounding himself with other believers. No wonder things were out of sorts.

You can't expect to be victorious in certain areas if you don't spend time with God in a disciple relationship. After recognizing that the reason he struggled so much was because of a lack of structured time with God, he made some much-needed changes. He began to attend church consistently. He was introduced to someone who was teaching a Bible study on campus, and he began to attend. From that Bible study, he began to attend a discipleship group, where he learned the real meaning of walking with God. You wouldn't believe the difference it made in his life. He said the one passage that really helped to turn things around was Psalm 119:11, "I have hidden your word in my heart that I might not sin against you." Studying God's Word and learning how to live according to it was the key to this student's turnaround.

One of the greatest examples of discipleship is found in Matthew 5–7, also known as the Sermon on the Mount, where

Jesus began to teach the disciples. After He gave the standards and expectations of living the Christian life, He ended with the importance of practicing what He had said.

> Therefore everyone who hears these words of mine and puts them into practice is like a wise man who built his house on the rock. The rain came down, the streams rose, and the winds blew and beat against that house; yet it did not fall, because it had its foundation on the rock. But everyone who hears these words of mine and does not put them into practice is like a foolish man who built his house on sand. The rain came down, the streams rose, and the winds blew and beat against that house, and it fell with a great crash. (Matthew 7:24–27)

Mark 3:14 says, "He appointed twelve—designating them apostles—that they might be with him and that he might send them out to preach." The disciples were with Jesus, being trained through instructions and practice. They were in continuous association and immediate fellowship with Jesus Himself. If you're going to be a disciple of Christ and learn to live by His commands, the only way to do this is to get time with Him through His Word, prayer, the church, Bible study, and other means and methods of fellowship. To live by the commands of Christ is truly to be His disciple.

CHAPTER NINETEEN

Sharing Our Faith

The Importance of Telling Others About Christ

This is the message we have heard from him and declare to you: God is light; in him there is no darkness at all.

—1 JOHN 1:5

R emember when you told everyone some good news you had, perhaps that you were going to college? Bet you couldn't wait to share the good news with everyone you knew. *Extra, extra, read all about it, I'm going to college!* Oh, it wasn't enough that you were going; you had to tell all the details about this great opportunity.

I can just hear you talking with your friends. "The school is in Knoxville, Tennessee. There are about thirty thousand students, and they have a great athletics program. The girls' basketball team always seems to compete for the National Championship. Who knows, I might walk on myself. I can't wait to get there."

I had that kind of enthusiasm about going to college. I realized how important going to college really is. It was the opportunity of a lifetime. When you grow up in poverty and the demand for goods exceeds the supply, getting a college education becomes the pot of gold at the end of the rainbow.

With college, I could finally do something to help my mom. I could do things for myself that before I could only dream about. I knew the sky was the limit for what I could do if I achieved a college education. The joy I had I couldn't keep to myself. I just had to share it with others. Such is the case when one comes to know Jesus Christ as Savior and Lord. It should be so important to you that you can't contain your joy. All of who He is causes you to want to tell others about a loving Savior.

During my freshman year at Troy State University, a campus minister who worked with the ministry of Campus Outreach told me the reasons that sharing my faith was important. I remember three things he said. First, he said that witnessing of my faith was a command from God. Second, in sharing my faith others may come to know Jesus Christ in a personal relationship. Finally, it was important because of the joy and satisfaction I would receive in doing so.

It has been some thirteen years since my college days ended. I am still motivated by these three life-changing facts. How about you—are you motivated by the fact that God commands you to tell others about Christ? Are you motivated by the possibilities that others may come to know Jesus Christ? Finally, do you realize that there is an almost unexplainable joy that overtakes you when you share your faith?

I guess the bottom line to what I was being told about sharing my faith was that, in doing so, I would be giving others the opportunity to know the greatest hope in all of yesterday, today, and tomorrow.

Over the years, I've developed my own list of reasons that sharing my faith is important. In Genesis 6 and 7 is the story of

Noah. I'm sure the story is familiar, but let me review some of its significant points. Genesis 6:8 says that Noah found favor in the eyes of the Lord. Noah was a righteous man, blameless in his time. We are told that the earth at this time was corrupt in the sight of God, and the earth was filled with violence. It kind of reminds me of the times we are living in right now.

The story continues with God's anger and ultimately His decision to destroy the earth. Noah was told by God to make an ark. God told Noah all the dimensions for building the ark. Finally God revealed His purpose to Noah. "I am going to bring floodwaters on the earth to destroy all life under the heavens, every creature that has the breath of life in it. Everything on earth will perish" (Genesis 6:17). Finally, Noah gathered his three sons, his wife, and his sons' wives. He also gathered two of every kind of animal, both male and female. They entered the ark, and, in the seventh day after they were aboard, God sent the rain.

The rain fell upon the earth forty days and forty nights. The waters were so great that they lifted the ark. It rose above the earth and began to float. The waters reached such a high level that not even the mountains were seen. Everything and everyone except those aboard the ark perished in this great flood.

What I find to be most intriguing is what I stumbled across in Matthew 24:37–39.

As it was in the days of Noah, so it will be at the coming of the Son of Man. For in the days before the flood, people were eating and drinking, marrying and giving in marriage, up to the day Noah entered the ark; and they knew nothing about what would happen until the flood came and took them all away. That is how it will be at the coming of the Son of Man.

Jesus Christ is the ark that floats amid the flood.

Another day of disaster is coming to the earth. The Bible tells us that it is going to rain again. Like Noah, you should be telling people it's going to rain, sharing with them the news about the only umbrella that can protect them in the storm. I believe according to God's Word that it's going to rain again—not with water but with fire. Is your umbrella ready?

CHAPTER TWENTY

The Word of God

Words to Live By

It is written: "Man does not live on bread alone, but on every word that comes from the mouth of God."
—MATTHEW 4:4

I know you probably do a lot of reading, but I would venture to say that you have never read anything quite like the Book God wrote. It almost seems too good to be true. In my personal pilgrimage, I've found that the Word of God speaks to every area and circumstance in my life. It comforts me when I am afraid. It gives me direction when I don't know where I am going. My needs are met because of its promises, and I just feel good when I read it. At times when I read it, I see places where I haven't been living according to God's best, and I see adjustments I need to make. Though that can be difficult, it keeps my life on track.

I will never forget being asked to read the gospel of John for the first time. John is one book that talks about the life of Jesus on earth. These are incredible words that have caused some of the greatest skeptics to believe. The master Teacher started meeting people and finding out who they were and revealing to them who He is. The most significant passage that jumped off the pages and melted my heart was John 3:16, "For God so loved the world that he gave his one and only Son, that whoever believes in him shall not perish but have eternal life."

What was three times illuminating was the word *whoever*. It doesn't matter who you are or where you've come from or how rich or poor you are. All that matters is that you are a *whoever*. That qualifies you to become a child of God. I came to the wonderful truth that the book of John was God's love story. John tells about many different people Jesus met and presented Himself to. Christ met them for the purpose of bringing salvation into their world and ours.

I learned quickly in college that most of my time was being spent reading and digesting words that only spoke to my mind and not to my heart. Words from books could only promise the possibility of getting a good job, but not the possibility of getting a crown. I don't mean to sound like I am belittling academics; I am not. School is necessary for acquiring knowledge and skills that can lead to opportunity. But there is a limit to what it can do.

While attending Troy State, I was told how important it was to have a standard to live by. I needed a filter that I could filter all of my decisions and circumstances through. Everything I did would pass through the filter of the Word. If it met the Bible standard, it made it through. If it didn't meet the biblical standard, it fell away. Everything had to line itself up next to the Word of God so that I could see exactly how to move from one place to the next.

I remember the first time I was challenged by a member of the college ministry I was involved with. I was only a freshman on campus, and I was growing in my relationship with Christ. Some members of the football team asked me to go to a local bar to just talk and maybe even have some drinks. I had gone out with them before, and I must say that I didn't feel all that comfortable. But I figured that it would be an innocent experience as long as I didn't drink or do some of the things they were doing. I wrestled with it for a long time until I was told to seek God's Word for the answers I needed. A staff member shared with me one particular passage that really opened my eyes.

Acts 1:8 says, "But you will receive power when the Holy Spirit comes on you; and you will be my witnesses in Jerusalem, and in all Judea and Samaria, and to the ends of the earth."

The key word for me was the word *witness.* I was told that God has called me to be a witness of His existence in my life. I determined that I wasn't being a very good witness by hanging out at the bar, where the atmosphere was negative and the people not in a mood to hear; therefore I declined their invitation to go.

Psalm 119, which is the longest chapter in the Bible, is presented to the reader as a devotional on the Word. The longest chapter is committed to one single theme, the Word. From the first verse to the last verse, the writer passionately expresses how devoted he is to the Word and how necessary the Word is. The key verse in Psalm 119 is verse 18. It says, "Open my eyes that I may see wonderful things in your law."

There truly are wonderful things in God's Word. If you can't see them, then you must pray so that God might open your eyes to them. If God doesn't open your eyes, you won't ever see the wonder, greatness, and life-changing power of His Word.

To those who can't see, these are just words on pages, but to those whose eyes God has opened, Christ has become the way to the very throne of God. Hey, you know that Bible that has been sitting on your dorm room shelf? Dust it off. Ask God in prayer to open your eyes, and get ready to be amazed.

CHAPTER TWENTY-ONE

Time to Pray

Why Prayer Is Important

Do not be anxious about anything, but in everything, by prayer and petition, with thanksgiving, present your requests to God. And the peace of God, which transcends all understanding, will guard your hearts and your minds in Christ Jesus.
—PHILIPPIANS 4:6–7

Hey, I hope you didn't get up this morning and forget to say your prayers. Better yet, I hope you didn't go to bed last night without saying your prayers. If you did, you missed out on the greatest privilege there is: the privilege of talking to God. If praying is something that you are getting used to, let me give you one of my secrets to developing a consistent prayer life. I was always told that prayer is important in the life of a Christian. Prayer is a way of communicating with God. I knew I had to start somewhere, so each night before I went to bed, I picked out the shoes I would wear to class the next day. I would take them and put them underneath my bed, way in the back. Lo and behold, I found myself on my knees. I figured that since I was down there, I might as well pray. The next morning, I would wake up, get on my knees, and reach for my shoes. Once again, it reminded me to take the time and pray. Of course, now I realize that I can pray while standing up, driving my car (as long as I keep my eyes open), or in any position or any place. But I knew that I needed to develop a habit of praying, and for me this was the reminder.

Some of the most wonderful experiences I've ever had were in getting together with other students on campus and praying. We knew that if we were going to hear from God, we needed to come together and pray. If there was going to be a movement on campus for Christ, it was important to lift up all the desires and things we wanted to see God do. We even made a list of requests so we could see how and when and in what way God would answer our prayers. Our list read like this: To see as many students as possible presented with the gospel. To have as many students as we could participate in our weekly campus meeting. To aggressively recruit students to our summer beach project for training. The list could almost be endless, but God was faithful and blessed us with answers to many of these requests.

Philippians 4:6–7 says, "Do not be anxious about anything, but in everything, by prayer and petition, with thanksgiving, present your requests to God. And the peace of God, which transcends all understanding, will guard your hearts and your minds in Christ Jesus."

Our campus prayer group also believed that it was important to pray for one another. Jesus was the ultimate model of intercessory prayer as He prayed to the Father on behalf of those who had sinned against God. In other words, Jesus Christ stood in the gap that separates you from God. He bridged it with His own life so our prayers could be heard.

Isaiah 53:12 says, "He bore the sin of many, and made intercession for the transgressors." What this really means is that you have made it this far because somebody prayed for you. Isn't that wonderful?

Our campus group also believed that prayer was important because of who God is. We liked to simply take the opportunity to revere Him because He is God all by Himself. He is in need of nothing and in want of nothing. He holds even your next breath in His hands. I could give you countless numbers of reasons that prayer is important; however, I must stop here, because at this very moment, I am going to drop this pencil and find me a nice quiet place and just thank God for even being able to recognize this wonderful privilege we call prayer.

Sorry that took so long. Where was I? Oh yeah, now I remember. I was talking about the importance of prayer.

Found in Acts 12:1–11 is the account of Peter's arrest and deliverance. Herod found it fitting to arrest Peter, placing him in prison and having him in maximum security to guard him. The Bible says that while Peter was kept in prison, the church of God was praying on his behalf. On the very night before the day that he was to be brought before Herod, Peter was found sleeping soundly in the jail cell. Now this is unusual because prison is no place to get comfortable, especially the night before you might be sentenced to death. An angel appeared and shook Peter to awaken him. The angel told Peter to follow him, and Peter did so, but he was uncertain whether or not he was dreaming. Finally, he recognized that God had released him from prison. On behalf of the prayers of others, Peter was freed.

■   ■   ■

Take a moment and stop reading this book. I want you to go somewhere quiet, calm, and peaceful and just have a moment to pray. Go have a little talk with Jesus.

PART FOUR

Arriving at Home
Being a Part of God's Family

Consequently, you are no longer foreigners and aliens, but fellow citizens with God's people and members of God's household.

—EPHESIANS 2:19

Take a moment and ponder what it means to be a part of a family. To me, the most important thing is that the family is a group of people who experience the joys and sorrows of life together. Your impressions of the family may stir up negative emotions that cause you to be angry, or they could bring positive emotions that cause you to be happy. Regardless of the perception, you have a unique tie or connection to each member of your family.

The roles and functions of each member are unique. The father leads and directs the family. The mother helps the father to be successful in his efforts. The children are being trained for eventual independence. And finally, there are other family members, cousins, uncles, aunts, and grandparents, who all play the supportive role in the family.

Beyond your birth family, however, there is the joy of being a part of God's family. Many benefits and privileges come with being a part of His family. The family that is saved together stays together. You might ask, "What is God's family?" Well, follow me in this final section and see what is yours as a child of the King.

CHAPTER TWENTY-TWO

A Family Affair
The Privilege of Being a Family Member

For this reason I kneel before the Father, from whom his whole family in heaven and on earth derives its name.

—EPHESIANS 3:14–15

Family reunion: a fun-filled affair that brings together family members from all over the country. They all migrate to one designated place. Some of them you know, but others you don't have a clue who they are. They come in all shapes and sizes. They are from every walk of life. Some are doctors. Others are lawyers, pastors, teachers, athletes, business professionals, and blue-collar workers. But most of all, and most important, they are all family. What a privilege it is to be a part of such a group of diverse people and see the many talents and gifts they all possess. What makes family reunions unique is that only family members are invited.

During my freshman year of college, my family began to make preparations for our family reunion. Letters were mailed out. Hotel reservations were made, and a whole lot of prayers were sent up. When three hundred family members get together, somebody had better be doing a lot of praying.

Now, my family is really strict about having nothing but family members attending family reunions. Guests or friends or anyone who was not a part of the family could not attend. My roommate in college heard all about the fun we had and all the things we did at our reunions. He was so impressed with some of my family ties that he wanted to come just to meet certain people. Unfortunately, I had to tell him my family was adamant about no one attending the reunion who was not a part of the family. Of course he understood, but he did request a few autographs and some pictures to verify my claims. Since he was my roommate and one of my best friends, I met his request. He couldn't believe the list of people who were tied to my family. He was in such awe with some of the members of my family that he wanted me to get him introduced at some later time.

After seeing his excitement about my family, I felt privileged to be a part of a family that he thought was so exciting. Though it is wonderful to be a part of the family I am part of, it's even more wonderful to be a member of the family of God.

Through accepting Jesus Christ as Lord and Savior, I have become a part of the family of God. Now that I am a member of His family, I am entitled to all the privileges a family member is allowed.

Ephesians I gives us a wonderful account of what we have due to our membership in God's family. First is the fact that God has blessed the believer with every spiritual blessing in Christ, meaning you and I have the kindness and favor of God upon our lives. Verse 7 tells us that we have been redeemed through the blood of Jesus Christ, that we have our sins forgiven and we no longer stand condemned to an eternal death. Verse 14 says we have an inheritance, meaning you and I as Christians will come into all that God has reserved in heaven for us. First Corinthians 2:9 says, "No eye has seen, no ear has heard, no mind has conceived what God has prepared for those who love him."

Think for a moment about all the things that you have seen in this life: beautiful beaches, fragile butterflies, craggy mountains, enormous homes, and wonderful cars. What about the things that have touched your heart and given you peace? If you are a member of God's family, nothing good you have experienced in this life even compares to what you will receive in the life to come.

Finally, in Ephesians 1:13–14, Paul says we have been sealed in Him with the Holy Spirit of promise, who is given as a pledge of our inheritance with a view to the redemption of God's own possession and His praise and glory. This means that the person of the Holy Spirit confirms us since we are Christians. And we are also made to be God's possessions. That means that because you are a member of His family, He owns you. You are His property. What a privilege to know that God has my life in His hands. And no one can ever take me out of His hands.

Romans 8:37–39 says:

In all these things we are more than conquerors through him who loved us. For I am convinced that neither death nor life, neither angels nor demons, neither the present nor the future, nor any powers, neither height nor depth, nor anything else in all creation, will be able to separate us from the love of God that is in Christ Jesus our Lord.

If you have accepted Jesus Christ, your relationship with Him can't be lost. You now have access to all of His assets. What is His is yours. Once in the family, always in the family. There isn't enough ink in all the pens in the world to record all of the wonderful privileges you have when you're in Jesus Christ. It's a family like no other. I can't wait to see all of the members of my godly family when I get to heaven. I assure you it will be like no reunion you have ever seen. Family membership does have its privileges.

CHAPTER TWENTY-THREE

The Power to Overcome

Being Plugged in to the Power Source

For God did not give us a spirit of timidity, but a spirit of power, of love and of self-discipline.
—2 TIMOTHY 1:7

Ever go to turn on the television only to discover that when you hit the power button, the TV didn't come on? You pressed it again, and still no power. First you thought there was something wrong with the television. Then you remembered the television was only a year old, so it probably wasn't the television. Finally, it hit you. Yesterday, you did some furniture rearranging, you unplugged the television so you could move it to another location, and you never plugged the cord back into the outlet. Now it made sense. No power, no movie. If you are going to watch that action-packed thriller, you'd better try plugging the TV back in. Pressing the power button on the television will do you no good if the television is receiving no power from the power source.

Each Christmas, I enjoy taking all of the Christmas lights out of their hibernation and setting them up around the house.

My wife gets a kick out of it because she waits for me to try to turn them on after setting them up. The lights I use all have a little mechanism with an on/off switch. Often the lights don't come on when I switch the mechanism to the *on* side. And I always stand there with a shocked look on my face, never realizing that the reason the lights didn't light up the house was that I failed to plug the cord into the outlet. Then I stand there completely amazed that I could forget the most important part of setting up the Christmas lights, plugging them in.

The power comes from the power source. With all the enormous temptations and peer pressure you face, as well as the daily struggles you may have with sometimes saying the wrong things or entertaining the wrong thoughts, sometimes just saying no when you need to say no can be difficult. Your friends ask you to go to the party scene, and you struggle to do what you know is the right thing. As a Christian, you have a power source in the person of the Holy Spirit, who lives inside of you. He is able to help you overcome all of the challenges and temptations and struggles that you experience on the college campus. When you are plugged into the power source, you have the power to be victorious come what may.

The book of Acts gives us some accounts of the presence of the Holy Spirit, demonstrating His work and power in the life of the Christian. Our connection to the Holy Spirit is like a power outlet. When you get plugged in to Him through accepting Jesus Christ as your Savior and Lord, you are then given power to overcome all that does not represent God's will for your life.

Acts 1:8 says, "But you will receive power when the Holy Spirit comes on you; and you will be my witnesses in Jerusalem, and in all Judea and Samaria, and to the ends of the earth." These were words spoken by Jesus Himself to His disciples, men who were being equipped to go into the world and reach the world with the good news of Jesus Christ. These were men who were plugged in to the source.

One example of the power of the Holy Spirit is taken from Acts 3. Peter and John, two of Jesus' disciples, were about to enter the temple to pray. A beggar who was born crippled was placed at the gate every day to beg for money. One day he saw Peter and John about to enter the temple and asked them for money. Peter and John looked at him, and Peter said, "Silver and gold I do not have, but what I have I give you" (v. 6). Peter told the man in the name of Jesus to walk. As he helped the man to his feet and the man's ankles got stronger, the man began to walk. The people who knew the man were amazed at what had happened. Peter and John certainly had within them the power of the Holy Spirit. They were plugged in to the power source of life.

God wants to give you, as He did Peter and John, the power to leave others amazed. What is even more amazing is that the power source that gave Peter and John the power to heal this crippled beggar is the same power source that lives within those who have accepted Jesus Christ as Lord and Savior.

You have within you as a Christian the greatest power source ever known to man. You don't have to live defeated. He, the Holy Spirit, gives you the power to overcome every circumstance. There are no thoughts that can't be controlled. There is no peer pressure that can't be defeated. There are no temptations that you can't escape. The power flows continuously, and there is always a supply of what you need when you need it.

I know what some of you are thinking. *What if the electric company turns the power off?* Well, they can't if you've paid the bill. And the power of the Holy Spirit can't be turned off either. Jesus Christ paid the bill two thousand years ago.

CHAPTER TWENTY-FOUR

A Solid Foundation

A Home Fit for the Storm

I will ask the Father, and he will give you another Counselor to be with you forever.

—JOHN 14:16

We've all had our fair share of storms. Usually the severity of a storm is determined by the damage left behind. The bigger the storm, the greater the damage. The smaller the storm, the less the damage. When it comes to natural disasters, the debate goes on and on. Which disaster is the worst? Is it a hurricane with its high tides, disastrous winds, and heavy rains? What about a tornado, which can destroy anything in its path, or what about an ice storm or a blizzard, which can destroy with its weight and kill with its cold and the slick surfaces it leaves?

The one that intrigues me the most is an earthquake. It is the only natural disaster by which the foundation can be destroyed. I don't know about you, but there's just something about the thought of the ground that holds me up moving out from underneath me that makes me think an earthquake might be the worst. These natural disasters can change the world in an instant.

■　　■　　　■

Before I got married, my wife, Stephanie, lived in Los Angeles for a few years after graduating from Auburn University. She packed her bags and went west. "We love LA!" was her favorite slogan. She was so pumped, going out there to pursue a dream. She wanted to make it big.

Well, she didn't feel the same sentiments after experiencing her first earthquake. Early one morning, she was awakened by a shaking that caused the furniture to be moved and the window glass to crack. She said it lasted for twelve seconds. The thing that frightened her the most was that she had nowhere to run. Everywhere she moved, the ground shook. Left or right, forward or backward, the ground shook. I can only imagine the horror. After twelve seconds of shaking, it was over. She calmed herself, took a deep breath, and thanked God she wasn't hurt.

Steph said there was no warning, as it is with earthquakes. They show up unannounced, whereas other storms or disasters can come with warnings. Tornadoes form funnel clouds, and storm cells are detected. Hurricanes can be picked up on weather radar. And you can always tell that if it rains too much there's a possibility of flooding. A guy named Noah can tell you about that. However, with earthquakes it could be today, it could be tomorrow.

During my senior year in college, a severe storm hit our campus. It was so bad that students were unable to attend class. Power lines fell to the ground. Trees were uprooted; winds were gusting at up to fifty miles per hour. Debris was flying everywhere. The damage left behind was really severe. The cleanup took two weeks.

Jesus says in Matthew 7:24–27:

> Therefore everyone who hears these words of mine and puts them into practice is like a wise man who built his house on the rock. The rain came down, the streams rose, and the winds blew and beat against that house; yet it did not fall, because it had its foundation on the rock. But everyone who hears these words of mine and does not put them into practice is like a foolish man who built his house on sand. The rain came down, the streams rose, and the winds blew and beat against that house, and it fell with a great crash.

When you have placed your faith in Christ, you have moved into a home that can't be blown down. The world may huff and puff, but it can't blow down the house of God. Storms are no match for God; with His help you can withstand any storm or disaster in this life.

Mark 4:35–41 tells us the story of Jesus calming an angry sea. I can't describe the mighty storm Jesus and the disciples were in, but it had to be quite a storm because the disciples were scared to death. (And several of them were fishermen.) Do you remember the movie *The Storm*, starring actor George Clooney? He played the role of a fisherman who sailed into the sea with a team of other fishermen in a desperate attempt to catch a lot of fish. After succeeding in their fishing, they found that there was a storm directly in the path that they were traveling to get home. It was a storm unlike anything you could imagine. It was very important to store the fish that they had caught on ice to preserve them. However, the ice machine aboard broke, and they were forced into the decision of sailing into the storm or waiting for it to pass and losing all their fish to spoilage. This was the way that these men made a living. If they were going to profit from their catch, they had to get the fish home. They decided to sail into the storm in hopes of making it through, but they were unsuccessful. The storm was so great that they got into waves as big as twenty-story buildings with winds exceeding one hundred miles an hour smashing up against their boat. Sadly, all aboard died in the mighty grip of a storm that wouldn't let go.

I believe Jesus and the disciples were caught in such a storm. The story tells us that Jesus was asleep in the stern of the boat, and the disciples woke Him and said to Him, "Teacher, don't you care if we drown?" (Mark 4:38). This cry for help woke Jesus, and He spoke calmly to the storm. He told the storm to be still—unlike the movie, where the fishermen had no one to calm the storm, no one to tell the wind to die down, no one to tell the water to get back, and no one to tell the crew not to be afraid.

When storms arise in your life, remember there's a Father who can calm the storm. He does care that you perish. He does care that you are afraid, and when you need Him, He is always there. All you have to do is tell Him that you're in a storm that is higher than your head. He may seem to be sleeping, because He isn't panicking along with you. But God is awake and waiting for you to ask.

CHAPTER TWENTY-FIVE

The Man of the House

A Father Who Cares

Cast all your anxiety on him because he cares for you.
—1 PETER 5:7

He rewards you when you accomplish something great. He disciplines you when you have done something wrong. He listens when you need an ear. He also knows and meets your needs. He's a father who cares. He's the man of the house.

Now that I have become a father, with two daughters of my own, it has been amazing to see how my children look to me for guidance. Let my youngest daughter tell the story, and I'm the best thing since sliced bread. Her daddy can do no wrong. You should hear her talk about her daddy to her schoolmates. "My daddy's muscles are really, really big." "My daddy lets me and my sister sit on his feet, and he walks us around the house and calls us his pair of shoes." "Every Wednesday he takes us out to the pan-a-cake store." (For those of you who don't know what the pan-a-cake store is, it's usually called the International House of

Pancakes, also known as IHOP. Ah yes, the Silver Dollar special. Five pancakes, two sausage links, and two scrambled eggs. And who can forget the hot maple syrup?) Somehow I've won their hearts.

I remember going to a college football game to watch one of the students I had been discipling while serving as campus director for the ministry of Campus Outreach. He was sure to remind me that his father was coming, and his father was looking forward to sitting with me at the game. The father had driven nearly six hours to see his son play. It seemed that he stood up for nearly the entire game, screaming at the top of his lungs. "Come on, guys, get with it." "We can win this game." "Don't give up; keep working." What a cheerleader. Even the fact that his son's team was beaten didn't dampen his enthusiasm and words of encouragement. "Maybe the next time." "Keep your head up; we've got seven games left." "Who knows, things could bounce our way next week." I guess the father recognized that the 5'11" 186-pound defensive back was more than just a football player. He was his son. And as a father who cares for his children, he was there to remind his son that Daddy understands.

Our heavenly Father also cares. He cares so much that He sent His Son, Jesus Christ, to die for you. The Father cares that you have fallen out of fellowship with Him through Adam. He cares that your sins needed forgiving. He cares about every little detail of your life. There's nothing too big or too small for the Father to care about.

Jesus gives us a wonderful account of how much God cares for you.

Therefore I tell you, do not worry about your life, what you will eat or drink; or about your body, what you will wear. Is not life more important than food, and the body more important than clothes? Look at the birds of the air; they do not sow or reap or store away in barns, and yet your heavenly Father feeds them. Are you not much more valuable than they? Who of you by worrying can add a single hour to his life? And why do you worry about clothes? See how the lilies of the field grow. They do not labor or spin. Yet I tell you that not even Solomon in all his splendor was dressed like one of these. If that is how God clothes the grass of the field, which is here today and tomorrow is thrown into the fire, will he not much more clothe you, O you of little faith? (Matthew 6:25–30)

The question was asked, How much does Jesus care for you? The answer: He stretched Himself wide on a wooden cross and said, "This much."

CHAPTER TWENTY-SIX

The Constant Provider

The God Who Meets All Our Needs

And my God will meet all your needs according to his glorious riches in Christ Jesus.

—PHILIPPIANS 4:19

Ever wonder where you'd be had your parents not provided all the things you needed? Food when you were hungry. Clothing when you were naked. Shelter when you needed a place to sleep. The very basic but necessary things you need to survive. Maybe you didn't get all that you wanted, but it's hard to argue that you didn't get all you needed. For many years, they have constantly met your needs. Sometimes you were ill and they took you to the doctor. When you fell and scraped your knee, they cleaned it up and put a bandage on it. From one thing to another, you were in need and they met the need.

Someone should give my mom an Oscar—she pulled off the performance of a lifetime. I didn't always know how she did it; all I knew was that when I was in need, she met the need. I don't think I ever realized how poor we were while growing up. But now that I've grown up, I know how bad it was, and man, were we poor. I can't tell you how many times my mom was working when we came home from school, and it seemed like there was nothing in the kitchen to eat. We would call Mom at work, and she would walk us through the kitchen on the phone and show us how to take what we thought was nothing in the kitchen and turn it into something.

We didn't always have the designer clothing that the other kids had, but the things that we had were more than enough. It wasn't always comfortable being in a two-bedroom, one-bathroom house, but it met our needs. The house was especially uncomfortable when my sister got the bathroom first. My brother and I just had to deal with it. My mom drove an old beat-up Ford, but it got us from place to place. Looking back, I can honestly say that all of our needs were met, and what was even more impressive was that my mom met them every day. She was a constant provider when I needed her the most.

I was so fortunate to have had an opportunity to go to college. I was blessed with a talent that opened the door for me to receive a scholarship. Before getting a scholarship, I knew that getting all my needs met in college would be a challenge. I didn't come from a home with a lot of money, and I didn't know anyone I could turn to for help with my tuition. However, through playing football, I was able to earn a full scholarship.

Of course, there were things I wanted while in college that I didn't get, but I certainly had everything I needed. I was going to need money to take care of room and board, and I had it. I was going to need money to pay for my books, and I had it. I had everything that I needed to make it four years on a college campus.

Philippians 4:19 says, "My God will meet all your needs according to his glorious riches in Christ Jesus."

I don't know what all of your needs are at this moment, but there is a provider who loves to meet every single need you have. The God of both heaven and earth is your constant provider. You won't always know how He's going to meet your needs, but He does. You can take complete comfort in the fact that He loves you enough to provide all the necessities in your life.

Jesus did many miraculous things during His time on earth to meet the needs of the people. One wonderful account is found in Matthew 14:13–21, where we are told that Jesus met a multitude of people who were sick, and He had compassion for them. He touched their sickness and healed them completely. Their need was to be healed, and so He healed them. Not only did He interact with people who needed healing, but also with those who needed food.

Once again He did the miraculous when He borrowed five loaves of bread and two fish. With them, He fed five thousand people. They said to Him, "We have here only five loaves of bread and two fish." And He said, "Bring them here to me." Jesus took the five loaves of bread and the two fish, prayed to heaven, and met the need of five thousand hungry people. In what is one of the most comforting chapters in the gospel, Jesus ultimately gave one of His greatest statements of provision. Jesus said in Matthew 6:26, "Look at the birds of the air; they do not sow or reap or store away in barns, and yet your heavenly Father feeds them. Are you not much more valuable than they?" People's greatest need is for a relationship with Him, and He meets that need for all who are willing.

God meets the needs of His children. Why? Because He loves us and we belong to Him.

CHAPTER TWENTY-SEVEN

Home Security
The God Who Protects

But the Lord is faithful, and he will strengthen and protect you from the evil one.
—2 THESSALONIANS 3:3

There's nothing like being safe in your own home. My wife made sure of that when we purchased the security alarm for our new home. A person couldn't enter the home without seeing the sign. It's attached to a two-foot iron pole with words that send a warning to all those who would dare try to break in. Little stickers in the windows serve as a reminder if the sign was overlooked. *Protected by Brinks Security.* The best alarm money can buy. There are two electronic keypads, monitoring sensors, motion detection devices, and at the push of a button immediate response from the authorities.

One particular summer our family went on a vacation. We packed our bags, stuffed them into the car, and did a last minute check of our house before departing. All systems were go, and all that was left to do was set the alarm. With the push of a button, the alarm was set, and off we went for seven glorious days in the Orlando sun. I would love to tell you all about the vacation, but that's another book. After just three days on our vacation, our neighbor contacted us and told us that there had been an attempted burglary at our home. It was only an attempt because the alarm was tripped upon entering our home, and the burglar was scared away. A police report had been filed, and therefore, we could finish our vacation and deal with the matter once we arrived home. The first words out of my wife's mouth were "Thank God for that alarm."

Late one night while sleeping in my college dorm, everyone was awakened by an incredibly loud alarm. I jumped out of my bed and ran to the door, opened it, and saw smoke down the hallway. Other students were making their way down the hall and out of the dorm. I quickly grabbed a pair of pants and headed out of the dorm. Fortunately, no one was hurt, and the small fire was quickly put out by the fire department.

The buzz on campus the next day was all about the fire. Who started it, and how did it start? Did anyone get hurt? How much damage was done? For me, I was just glad that there were alarms in the dorms to wake the students up. There's no greater protection than having a fire alarm in the event of a fire. It was security worth having.

First Peter 1:3–5 says:

Praise be to the God and Father of our Lord Jesus Christ! In his great mercy he has given us new birth into a living hope through the resurrection of Jesus Christ from the dead, and into an inheritance that can never perish, spoil or fade—kept in heaven for you, who through faith are shielded by God's power until the coming of the salvation that is ready to be revealed in the last time.

That means if you are saved, you are shielded and your salvation is kept from the moment you first believed. You are in a continual growing process, but when Christ returns, He will complete the salvation process through glorification. You can be sure that nothing that comes upon you can take away that pure salvation that God has granted through His Son, Jesus Christ. You are secure in the home of God. You are protected and shielded by His presence. Nothing can separate us from the love of God. Nor can anyone or anything remove the salvation that He has granted us.

Found in Romans 8:28–39 is the account of the security of the believer. Paul tells us that the work of salvation is entirely the work of God and thus is sustained by God through the shed blood of Jesus Christ. Paul leaves us with an incredible confirmation of how secure are those who have placed faith in Jesus Christ. He says in Romans 8:35–39:

> Who shall separate us from the love of Christ? Shall trouble or hardship or persecution or famine or nakedness or danger or sword? As it is written: "For your sake we face death all day long; we are considered as sheep to be slaughtered." No, in all these things we are more than conquerors through him who loved us. For I am convinced that neither death nor life, neither angels nor demons, neither the present nor the future, nor any powers, neither height nor depth, nor anything else in all creation, will be able to separate us from the love of God that is in Christ Jesus our Lord.

A little home security can go a long way when you need peace of mind. Don't worry. God is armed and ready.

CHAPTER TWENTY-EIGHT

And the Greatest of These

The God Whose Motivation Is Love

This is love: not that we loved God,
but that he loved us and sent his Son
as an atoning sacrifice for our sins.
—1 JOHN 4:10

Why do you suppose that your parents or guardians have given their time, resources, and work to your development and nurturing? One reason is that they are driven by love—unconditional love that reaches beyond your stubbornness, beyond your disobedience, and wraps its arms around you. They have probably made countless sacrifices so you would have opportunity. What love!

As I look back at the sacrifices my mom made for me, I stand amazed. To really grasp the impact of her love for me is incredible. Rising early to catch the bus to work. Standing in the morning cold during the winter. Walking in the smoldering heat during the summer. Taking little and stretching it to provide something to eat.

After being on her feet all day, Mom's tired feet would sometimes swell to the point of her not being able to walk. I remember soaking her feet in warm water and massaging them to bring
some level of relief. She sometimes washed our clothes with her
bare hands and dried them by hanging them on doors and pieces
of furniture throughout the house. For eighteen years of my life
I saw her give herself away to me for one purpose: I was hers and
she loved me because I was. I had nothing to give. I was strictly a
receiver. She gave and I received. She prepared the meals, and I
ate them. She cleaned the clothes, and I wore them. She em-
braced the pain, and I received the gain. What can I say? She
loves me.

Your wanting to succeed in college and in life should honor
the fact that your parents or guardians have probably given their
all to see you have an opportunity of a lifetime. Why did they
give? Because they love you. Love drives thousands of miles to
visit you on weekends (or at least calls you once in a while). Love
writes those checks that pay your tuition and room and board, or
encourages you as you work to put yourself through, and love
stands up for you when everyone else sits down. What can you
say? They love you.

As great as the love of a parent is, it pales in comparison to
the love that God has demonstrated toward you through Jesus
Christ, His only Son. John 3:16 says, "For God so loved the
world that He gave His only begotten Son that whoever believes
in Him shall not perish, but have eternal life" (NASB). God gave
His only Son because He loves you. He loves you perfectly, and
He loves you continuously. The songwriter said it best, "Jesus
loves me this I know. For the Bible tells me so. Little ones to
Him belong, they are weak but he is strong. Yes, Jesus loves me.
Yes, Jesus loves me. Yes, Jesus loves me. The Bible tells me so."

The Bible is God's love story about a Savior who would come to restore and redeem a fallen people. You and I are those fallen people.

The Bible in its entirety communicates God's love for you. From Genesis to Revelation, the hound of heaven comes after you relentlessly. He is looking for you. He wants to wrap His arms around you and whisper the sweetest words the human ear will ever hear: I love you! First John 4:16 says, "We know and rely on the love God has for us. God is love. Whoever lives in love lives in God, and God in him."

The apostle Paul gives us one of the greatest perspectives of love in the entire Bible. The Corinthian people were having a hard time understanding what God's expectations of them were. Paul, in his first letter to them, was careful to express that all of their talents and gifts meant nothing unless their motivation was love.

God's motive today is still love. The reason God won't ever give up on you is that He loves you. The reason that He keeps putting people in your path who reveal the character of God is that He loves you. The reason He continues to be faithful in spite of your unfaithfulness is that He loves you.

God, with every ounce of His being, loves you. Don't ever forget it.

Well, it's time for my writing journey with you to end. Thanks for going on the great adventure with me. I am certain you have a lot to think about.

Remember, He loves you so much that one day His Son, Jesus Christ, is going to return to get you and take you to be with Him. I hope your bags are packed. Mine are. It's almost time to go home.

Final Thoughts

Well, we've come to the end of the road. At this very moment, I can hear my wife calling me to read the girls a bedtime story. But before I go, I need to leave you with this final thought. The road from here to there starts here, with the undeniable fact that you and I were born into sin. We were separated from God and enemies of the Cross. But God who is rich in mercy has cut a path from our sins to His Son. A path that leads to the Cross.

In the movie *The Wizard of Oz*, Dorothy, in her effort to get home, knew that if she could just talk with the great and powerful Oz, her dreams of going home would become reality. "Follow the yellow brick road," everyone proclaimed. It leads to the great Oz. Dorothy followed the yellow brick road, and it got her as far as Kansas. If you and I want to get home, there is no yellow brick road. There is, however, a road that is paved with the blood of the crucified Jesus. Those who follow that road will find themselves there—at the Cross where all sins are washed away. What an adventure! What a Savior! Good night!

Since 1894, Moody Publishers has been dedicated to equip and motivate people to advance the cause of Christ by publishing evangelical Christian literature and other media for all ages, around the world. Because we are a ministry of the Moody Bible Institute of Chicago, a portion of the proceeds from the sale of this book go to train the next generation of Christian leaders.

If we may serve you in any way in your spiritual journey toward understanding Christ and the Christian life, please contact us at www.moodypublishers.com.

"All Scripture is God-breathed and is useful
for teaching, rebuking, correcting and training in
righteousness, so that the man of God may be
thoroughly equipped for every good work."
—*2 Timothy 3:16, 17*

MOODY
PUBLISHERS

THE NAME YOU CAN TRUST®

THE GREAT ADVENTURE TEAM

ACQUIRING EDITOR:
Greg Thornton

DEVELOPMENTAL EDITOR:
Joan Guest

COPY EDITOR:
Cheryl Dunlop

BACK COVER COPY:
Julie-Allyson Ieron, Joy Media

COVER DESIGN:
Ragont Design

INTERIOR DESIGN:
Ragont Design

PRINTING AND BINDING:
Color House Graphics Inc.

The typeface for the text of this book is
Centaur MT